SCALING
SMART

TIMELESS LEADERSHIP
PRINCIPLES FOR
SCALABLE SUCCESS

ROBERT ANDERSON, JR.

FREILING
AGENCY

Published by Freiling Agency, LLC.

P.O. Box 1264
Warrenton, VA 20188

www.FreilingAgency.com

PB ISBN: 978-1-963701-46-3
HB ISBN: 978-1-963701-47-0
E-book ISBN: 978-1-963701-48-7

CONTENTS

Introduction...v

1   Learn to Lead Before You Scale.........................1

2   Scaling Your Vision Before Scaling Your
     Company..19

3   The Leadership Blind Spot – Learning How to
     Listen..29

4   Providing Value – The True Measure of Scaling
     Success...49

5   I Need Help – The Power of Seeking Support in
     Scaling Success..63

6   Creeping Excellence – The Power of Continuous
     Improvement in Scaling Success.......................81

7   Power vs. Control – How Leadership Drives
     Scaling Success..99

8   Never Quit Attitude – The Resilience Required
     to Scale..113

9   Virtual Leadership – Leading and Scaling in a
     Remote World 125

10   Emotional Intelligence – The Hidden Driver of
     Scaling Success..135

11   Dealing with Change – Embracing the
     Inevitable 151

12   Motivational Speaking – Inspiring Action
     Through Communication 163

13   Looking Ahead..179

INTRODUCTION

All businesses evolve through three distinct stages: Launch, Sustain, and Scale. Starting a business is undeniably hard—it requires a bold vision, relentless effort, and often limited resources to transform an idea into a reality. The harsh reality is that most businesses never really get off the ground, falling victim to challenges like insufficient capital, poor planning, or an inability to gain traction in a competitive market. The launch phase is where dreams are tested, and only those with determination and a clear strategy can push through to the next stage.

If you survive the grand opening, the real challenges begin, and they only get harder. Running a business isn't just about getting through the initial excitement; it's about sustaining operations over the long haul. It demands consistency in delivering value to your customers, maintaining quality, and meeting expectations every single day. Operational efficiency becomes crucial as you juggle limited resources, tight budgets, and the pressure to optimize processes. On top of that, you're constantly navigating the day-to-day complexities of managing employees, addressing customer concerns, staying ahead of competitors, and adapting to market shifts—all while keeping the lights on and the business afloat. The honeymoon phase of launching fades quickly, replaced by the relentless grind of ensuring your business can survive and thrive in an ever-changing environment.

Let's say you make it this far. Congratulations! You've already achieved what many can't—you've moved past the launch phase and established a sustainable business. You're now part of the upper 10%, the select few who can confidently say they are successful founders. It's still not easy work, but it's no longer a start-up. It's a keep-going! This is harder than you think, which is partly why I wrote this book.

What next? At this stage, the focus shifts from mere survival to building organizational resilience and efficiency. You've proven you can create something lasting, but now the real question is: can you take it to the next level? Scaling smartly will determine whether your success is temporary or you can grow into something truly extraordinary.

However, scaling is by far the hardest stage of all. Scaling means growing bigger and doing so in a way that doesn't break the organization. It's where leaders must expand capacity, maintain culture, and ensure systems are robust enough to handle increased demands. Each stage builds on the previous one, but scaling requires a level of foresight, strategy, and adaptability that challenges even the most experienced leaders. It's where businesses are made—or broken. That's where this book begins.

If you ask CEOs about scaling, their eyes light up with excitement. They eagerly share metrics like skyrocketing revenue growth, expanding market share, or acquiring throngs of new customers. They talk about aggressive sales strategies, breaking into new markets, and outpacing competitors in their industry. Scaling, for many, represents the ultimate measure of success—a testament to their leadership and vision. They view it as an opportunity to solidify their position in the market and achieve exponential growth.

Indeed, scaling a business is one of the most exciting milestones for any leader—but again, it's also where many organizations fail.

In most cases, scaling revolves around growth as a goal rather than the strategy and infrastructure required to achieve and sustain it. But the truth is that most companies aren't prepared for the challenges that come with growth. Exhilaration is followed by chaos when the demands of rapid growth outpace the organization's ability to handle it. Processes break down, communication falters, and teams become overwhelmed, leaving leaders scrambling to fix unexpected problems. What starts as an exciting opportunity often turns into a struggle for survival.

Here's the problem with how many business leaders think about scaling: while fast revenue growth is an important aspect of scaling, leaders tend to emphasize the visible outcomes—the growth itself—rather than the underlying processes that make sustainable scaling possible. Rarely do leaders consider the foundational elements like creating scalable systems, nurturing a strong company culture, or ensuring their team is equipped to handle the increased complexity that comes with growth.

This surface-level thinking reveals a common blind spot: seeing scaling as a destination rather than a deliberate and carefully managed process. Scaling isn't just about doing more; it's about doing better in a way that sets the organization up for long-term success. It isn't just about growing bigger—it's about growing smarter.

This book will dive into the principles and practices that help leaders build scalable systems, foster a resilient culture, and navigate the complexities of sustainable growth. It's about equipping you with the leadership tools to scale with permanence. It takes more than effective management to scale your business; it takes effective leadership.

Now, you might be thinking: I don't need to scale. I'm happy where I'm at. The truth is that scaling is essential for long-term success and sustainability—it's how businesses evolve to meet new challenges and seize new opportunities.

When I meet a CEO or a business leader who doesn't take smart scaling seriously, I remind them that their business risks stagnation and will eventually become irrelevant in an increasingly competitive market. You'll eventually find yourself unable to meet growing customer demand, leading to dissatisfaction and lost opportunities. Your competitors, who are scaling effectively, will outpace you by offering better products or faster services. Internally, your team might become overburdened as they try to manage growth without the necessary systems and resources, leading to burnout and turnover. Financially, you'll plateau, unable to leverage economies of scale to increase profitability. Over time, staying static in a dynamic environment can erode your market share, damage your reputation, and leave your business vulnerable to disruption by more agile competitors.

Don't believe it? We see evidence of non-smart scaling all around us. Many companies have failed to scale effectively, leading to their decline or collapse. Pets.com, for instance, expanded rapidly without a sustainable business model, leading to its liquidation just months after its IPO. Once a global leader in mobile phones, Nokia struggled to innovate and scale in response to the smartphone revolution, losing its market dominance. Blockbuster, a giant in video rentals, failed to adapt its model to the digital streaming era, allowing competitors like Netflix to overtake the market. Similarly, BlackBerry, known for its iconic smartphones with physical keyboards, could not scale and innovate fast enough to compete with touchscreen devices, leading to its decline. Even retail giant Sears, once a household name, failed to scale and adapt in the face of e-commerce and discount retail competitors, resulting in store closures and bankruptcy. These examples underscore the importance of scaling smartly and adapting to market changes to ensure long-term success.

The pitfalls of non-smart scaling are not just cautionary tales—they are a call to action for leaders in any sector. Avoiding these mistakes requires more than just an awareness of the risks; it demands hands-on experience and a deep understanding of what it takes to grow sustainably. Scaling isn't theoretical—it's a practical, lived challenge that tests every aspect of leadership and strategy. Having witnessed these failures and their consequences, I approached scaling with the lessons I learned from a career in both public service and the private sector, where the stakes of growth are just as high but take on different forms. My journey through these challenges has shaped my understanding of what it means to scale smartly.

What do I know about scaling a business? I've lived it as a leader in both the public and private sectors. After a long and distinguished career at the Federal Bureau of Investigation (FBI)—where I served as Executive Assistant Director, overseeing global criminal, cyber investigations, international operations, and critical incidents—I made the leap to the private sector. I ran a large practice in a multi-billion dollar consultancy, I performed senior-level advisory roles to global businesses abroad before I stepped into the role of CEO at a fledgling cybersecurity company. I was determined to transform it into one of the world's leading firms. It was an ambitious, even audacious goal, but I've never been one to shy away from thinking big and tackling challenges head-on.

Stepping into the private sector, I quickly learned that scaling a business comes with its own set of unique challenges—ones that even my extensive experience at the FBI hadn't fully prepared me for. In the early days, I faced the reality of what happens when growth outpaces preparation. Systems that worked for a small operation couldn't handle the demands of rapid expansion, and I saw firsthand how quickly cracks could form in areas like communication, team alignment, and operational efficiency.

Fortunately, my team and I learned fast and embraced the need to pivot when necessary. By fostering a culture of adaptability and focusing relentlessly on execution, we were able to transform challenges into opportunities. The result was extraordinary: we scaled revenue and profit by more than 200% in less than three years, laying the groundwork for sustained success and future growth. It didn't come without pain, but nothing does. These experiences taught me invaluable lessons about the importance of building scalable systems, fostering a resilient culture, and staying disciplined amid the chaos of growth. Scaling wasn't just a business challenge—it became a personal journey of leadership, adaptability, and learning.

But I'm not the only CEO who's run into brick walls while scaling a business. It's altogether too common. Research indicates that 74% of high-growth internet startups fail due to premature scaling—expanding operations before establishing a solid foundation. Additionally, data shows that 38% of startup failures are attributed to financial issues, such as running out of cash or failing to raise new capital, often exacerbated by attempts to scale too quickly. Indeed, I'm not alone. Statistics underscore the critical importance of scaling smartly, ensuring sustainable growth, and supported by robust systems and resources.

FROM FBI TO CEO:
A JOURNEY OF LEADERSHIP

As I just shared, my story begins in an entirely different arena than a fast-growing business. I started in 1987 as a Delaware State Trooper, and eventually, in 1995, I became a Special Agent in the Federal Bureau of Investigation (FBI). During my tenure at the FBI, I led critical investigations into some of the most high-profile cases in modern history. The stakes were always high, often involving matters of national security or protecting critical infrastructure, which demanded resilience under pressure and the ability to make tough calls in real-time.

These experiences weren't just lessons in national security—they were lessons in leadership under pressure, at scale. Managing teams of highly skilled professionals, making decisions with incomplete information and ensuring the mission's success was all part of the job. And the job was achieved with more than 35,000 employees.

Scaling at the FBI, and in the government in general, isn't about increasing its size or creating new divisions; it's about expanding its capacity to respond to evolving threats and challenges without losing focus on its mission. As a leader there, scaling meant ensuring our teams could handle new, unprecedented problems—like cyber intrusions and insider threats—while still maintaining operational excellence in traditional areas like counterterrorism and criminal investigations. It required fostering agility in a system that could easily stagnate under bureaucracy, adapting quickly to emerging priorities, and developing scalable systems for managing resources and talent.

So, when I transitioned to the private sector, I brought a wealth of scaling experience that could translate to the private sector and also an unshakable resolve. But again, the shift wasn't without its challenges. Moving from a hierarchical government organization to the dynamic world of private enterprise required me to adapt my leadership style, learn the nuances of corporate culture, and embrace the rapid pace of technological change. Scaling meant something different.

SCALING IS MISUNDERSTOOD

Many equate scaling with growth, but the two are not synonymous. Growth is about adding resources—more people, products, and revenue. Scaling, on the other hand, is about adding capacity to support sustainable growth. It's about building an organization that can handle increased demands without compromising its core values, culture, or operational efficiency.

Here's how I like to think about it: a house built on a weak foundation may stand for a while, but it will crumble when subjected to the pressures of time and nature. Similarly, an organization that grows without scaling smartly risks collapsing under its own weight. Scaling smartly reinforces that foundation—creating systems and processes that allow the organization to thrive under pressure.

Unlike most books about scaling, which focus on the tactical aspects of expansion—such as financial modeling, marketing strategies, or operational efficiencies—this book takes a different approach. Scaling is not just about logistics and execution; it's about leadership. The ability to scale smartly is not determined solely by a company's systems and strategies but by the leaders' strength, vision, and adaptability guiding that growth. Many organizations fail not because they lack a growth plan but because their leaders are not equipped to manage the complexities that come with expansion.

This book is about the foundational leadership principles required for successful scaling. It's not about managing the process of scaling but leading people through it. A company's systems and structures can only take it so far; the real determinants of sustainable growth are its leaders' decisions, behaviors, and mindset. Leaders who focus solely on business mechanics without developing their leadership skills will find themselves struggling to maintain alignment, culture, and engagement as their organization grows. In contrast, those who build strong leadership capabilities will find that scaling happens more naturally because they have created an environment where people are inspired, engaged, and equipped to handle the challenges of growth.

The difference between managing and leading becomes even more pronounced when an organization begins to scale. Managing is about maintaining order, overseeing processes, and optimizing efficiency. Leading is about setting direction, empowering teams, and making the hard choices that define an organization's future. Scaling requires more than operational expertise; it requires courage, clarity, and the ability to inspire others to embrace growth as a shared mission. In the chapters ahead, we will explore the essential leadership principles that separate those who scale smartly from those who scale recklessly—and how mastering these principles will determine whether an organization thrives or collapses under the weight of its own ambition.

So this book is not about offering cookie-cutter solutions or abstract theories. Instead, it provides a practical, real-world leadership framework for scaling an organization. The principles outlined here are rooted in my experiences and designed to be actionable and adaptable. The foundation of sustainable scaling isn't just about operations—it's about leadership. Here are the 10 core tenets of the **Scaling Smart Leadership** framework, which I'll share in this book:

Listen – Everything begins with listening. Leaders who fail to listen to their employees, customers, and market signals will struggle to make informed decisions. Effective scaling requires leaders who actively seek input, encourage open communication, and identify blind spots before they become roadblocks.

Providing Value – Scaling isn't about growth for growth's sake. True, sustainable expansion happens when an organization consistently delivers value. Companies that scale smartly focus on enhancing customer experience, improving their products or services, and maintaining relevance in their industry.

I Need Help – No leader can scale an organization alone. Admitting that you need help—whether from mentors, advisors, or your own team—is a sign of strength, not weakness. Leaders who delegate, seek expertise, and foster collaboration are the ones who scale effectively.

Creeping Excellence – The best organizations don't scale overnight; they evolve through a continuous pursuit of improvement. "Creeping excellence" is the idea that small, incremental raising of standards compound over time, above what is required.

Power vs. Control – Scaling requires leadership, not micromanagement. Leaders who seek control over every aspect of the business will inevitably slow down growth. The right approach is to empower employees with decision-making authority while maintaining strategic oversight.

Never Quit Attitude – Resilience is a defining trait of leaders who successfully scale their organizations. There will be setbacks, challenges, and moments of uncertainty, but the ability to persist and adapt in the face of adversity determines long-term success.

Virtual Leadership – In today's increasingly remote and hybrid work environments, scaling requires mastering virtual leadership. Communication, culture-building, and maintaining alignment across dispersed teams are essential skills for modern leaders looking to scale beyond geographical constraints.

Emotional Intelligence – The larger an organization becomes, the more critical emotional intelligence (EI) becomes. Leaders who can navigate interpersonal dynamics, build trust, and manage their own emotions effectively will create stronger teams and foster a culture of accountability and collaboration.

Dealing with Change – Scaling is change. Leaders who embrace change, rather than resist it, will position their organizations to remain agile and competitive. Managing change effectively requires clear communication, a structured transition plan, and an ability to keep teams aligned amid uncertainty.

Motivational Speaking – A leader's ability to communicate their vision and inspire their team is crucial for scaling. Whether addressing employees, investors, or customers, leaders must master the art of storytelling, persuasion, and motivation to drive collective action.

While these principles are essential for scaling, they are rarely what most leaders immediately associate with the concept. When leaders think about scaling, they often fixate on tangible metrics like revenue growth, market expansion, or customer acquisition. They envision scaling as an external endeavor driven by sales, marketing, and product proliferation rather than an internal transformation.

What they overlook is that true scaling isn't just about outward-facing growth—it's about creating a foundation strong enough to sustain it. Without integrating these core elements, scaling efforts often falter, leading to organizational strain, misalignment, and eventual failure. Scaling smartly requires leaders to shift their perspective, focusing on where the organization is going and how it's prepared to get there.

A ROADMAP FOR SUCCESS

Scaling smartly is not a destination; it's a journey. It's a continuous process of learning, adapting, and evolving. This book is a roadmap for that journey, providing the tools and insights you need to navigate the challenges ahead. As you read through the chapters, you'll encounter stories from my career, case studies from other organizations, and actionable strategies for scaling your own business.

Whether you're an entrepreneur bootstrapping your first startup or a seasoned executive managing a large corporation, the challenges of scaling remain daunting. My goal is not just to inspire you but to equip you with the knowledge and confidence to take your organization to the next level.

Leadership in today's world requires courage, resilience, and a willingness to embrace change. But the rewards of smart scaling are worth the effort. By building a resilient and dynamic organization, you can create lasting impact—not just for your business but for the people it serves. Remember that scaling is not just about achieving financial success. It's about creating something meaningful, something that stands the test of time. It's about leading with purpose and making a difference.

Welcome to *Scaling Smart*. Let's get started.

1

LEARN TO LEAD BEFORE YOU SCALE

B efore I share the leadership principles that will help guide you through a successful scale, I want to begin by emphasizing a fundamental truth: you need to learn to lead before you scale.

Too many entrepreneurs and executives assume that leadership is something they can figure out along the way—that once they reach a certain size, they'll adapt and grow into the role. But scaling doesn't create great leaders; it exposes them. The pressures of expansion, the increasing complexity of decision-making, and the growing demands of a larger team will magnify every weakness, every gap in your leadership approach, and every hesitation you've ignored. If you haven't built the foundation of strong leadership before scaling, you won't have the skills, resilience, or clarity to sustain growth when challenges arise. Scaling is not just about increasing numbers—it's about expanding capacity, strengthening your ability to inspire, and ensuring that your organization remains stable and aligned as it grows. Leadership isn't something you put off until later; it's the skill that will determine whether your scale is sustainable or short-lived.

Scaling a business is an exhilarating milestone that leaders often rush toward with the best intentions but without the necessary preparation. The reality is that scaling too soon or without the right foundation can be more damaging than not scaling at all. Before a company even considers expanding, it must undergo an honest, unfiltered assessment of its readiness. The pre-scale phase lays the groundwork, where potential pitfalls are identified and addressed before they become an unmanageable crisis.

This was a lesson I had to learn quickly when I transitioned from the public sector to the private sector. When I first stepped into the private sector, I was eager to make an impact and prove that we could take the company to the next level. My mindset was simple: scale fast, sell hard. If we could increase our sales velocity, everything else would fall into place. With that in mind, I set out to build the strongest sales team in the industry. I recruited top talent, bringing in high-performing sales professionals from major firms. I wanted closers, people who could land deals and drive revenue immediately. I was relentless in this pursuit, convinced that more sales meant more success.

As a result, we expanded our sales department at an aggressive pace, pushing forward with an almost singular focus on growth. We implemented ambitious quotas, launched aggressive outreach strategies, and doubled down on lead generation. The energy was electric, and for a while, it seemed like we were on the right track. But I failed to see at the time that while we were accelerating sales, we weren't reinforcing the systems that supported that growth. We were scaling without structure, and cracks started forming beneath the surface. The rush to expand was exhilarating, but the foundation wasn't ready to support the weight of that growth.

The company wasn't ready to scale, and instead of growing, we were stagnant with a worse bottom line. Despite early successes, we were at a critical juncture where every decision we made would shape the company's trajectory for years to come. On the surface, we had momentum—our client base was growing, revenue was increasing, and there was a buzz around what we were building. But beneath that momentum lay deeper questions that we hadn't fully addressed. Were our operational processes strong enough to handle a surge in demand? Could our culture withstand the pressures of rapid expansion without fracturing? Did we have the right leadership structure in place to guide us through the complexities of scaling?

These fundamental concerns would determine whether we built a sustainable business capable of long-term growth or pushed forward prematurely and risked collapsing under our own ambitions. The excitement of growth was intoxicating, but growth without preparation was dangerous. The answer to our future depended entirely on how well we managed the pre-scale phase—not just as an operational necessity but as a strategic imperative that would separate lasting success from a cautionary tale of premature expansion.

THE FBI'S APPROACH TO SCALING

Interestingly, I had already encountered these same challenges in an entirely different arena—the Federal Bureau of Investigation. The FBI may not be a corporation, but in many ways, it operates like one, particularly when it comes to scaling its capabilities in response to emerging threats. Growth within the Bureau isn't just about adding more agents or increasing budget allocations; it's about ensuring that expansion strengthens operational effectiveness rather than overwhelming the system.

The FBI isn't much different than any other government-run organization. They all occasionally face a need to scale, which they do. On the surface, the expansion could seem like progress, but internally, it could create significant growing pains. Infrastructure could lag behind the rapid increase in personnel. Communication silos form, complicating coordination between new and existing teams. Leadership has to rapidly adapt to an organization that is transforming before their eyes. More employees don't automatically mean better outcomes. More resources don't always translate to efficiency.

The same principle applies to businesses. Growth for the sake of growth is not a strategy; it's a gamble. Unless leaders commit to a pre-scale process—ensuring that operations, culture, and leadership structures can withstand expansion—they're not truly scaling. They're simply accelerating toward potential disaster.

More people do not necessarily mean better. Adding more staff to a project does not necessarily lead to increased efficiency or faster completion. This concept is encapsulated in Brooks's Law, which states that "adding manpower to a late software project makes it later." Fred Brooks introduced this idea in his 1975 book, *The Mythical Man-Month*, highlighting that new team members require time to become productive and that increased personnel can lead to higher communication overhead, potentially hindering progress. Therefore, organizations must assess their specific needs and existing team dynamics before deciding to expand their workforce.

THE ILLUSION OF READINESS

Just because a company is stable does not mean it's ready to scale. Yet, like many organizations, there was a strong internal push to expand aggressively—more clients, more revenue, more markets. The enthusiasm was understandable. Everyone wants to be part of a growth story. But when I took a step back and analyzed the problem from a pre-scale perspective, I saw red flags that couldn't be ignored.

1. **Operational Fragility** – Our processes were functional but not scalable. The systems in place worked well for a small, agile team, but they weren't built to withstand the pressures of rapid expansion.

2. **Cultural Stability** – Company culture is often overlooked when leaders talk about scaling. However, a strong culture acts as the glue that holds everything together during times of growth. We had a dedicated team in several practices and companies, but the culture hadn't yet been stress-tested in a high-growth environment.

3. **Customer-Centric Infrastructure** – Scaling a business isn't just about bringing in more customers; it's about ensuring the business can support them without compromising quality or service. We needed a customer experience strategy that could scale with us.

4. **Leadership Alignment** – Many organizations assume that just because a leadership team functions well at one stage, it will function just as well at the next. This is rarely the case. Scaling requires leaders to evolve, delegate more effectively, and anticipate challenges they've never faced before.

These were all issues that, if ignored, would have turned scaling into a liability rather than an opportunity. Expanding too quickly without addressing these foundational gaps would have meant exposing the business to operational bottlenecks, employee burnout, customer dissatisfaction, and financial instability—all of which could have been fatal to our long-term success. Scaling is not just about getting bigger; it's about ensuring that growth is sustainable, that the systems in place can support increased complexity, and that the culture remains intact as the company evolves.

So, instead of jumping into growth mode, we pressed pause and focused on strengthening the foundation. We took a hard look at our operational processes, identified weak points, and streamlined workflows to eliminate inefficiencies. We reinforced our leadership team, ensuring we had the right people in the right positions to guide the organization through the challenges ahead. We stress-tested our company culture, ensuring it could withstand the pressures of scaling without losing its core values. Most importantly, we created a strategic roadmap for growth—one that was methodical, intentional, and built on a solid infrastructure. By preparing before scaling, we positioned ourselves to grow smarter, not just faster.

THE PRE-SCALE CHECKLIST

One thing I learned from my government experiences and in private sector leadership is that every organization must conduct a rigorous pre-scale assessment before committing to growth. Scaling a business isn't just about expanding operations or increasing revenue—it's about ensuring that the entire organization is structurally prepared to handle the additional complexity that comes with growth. Scaling can lead to operational breakdowns, cultural erosion, and financial instability without the right foundation. Below are the critical steps that should never be skipped in the pre-scale phase.

STRENGTHEN THE CORE OPERATIONS

A business should never attempt to scale if its internal operations are fragile. Scaling magnifies inefficiencies, and what might seem like minor operational weaknesses at a smaller size can quickly spiral into major obstacles as the business grows. Before expanding, leaders must conduct a comprehensive audit of all business processes—everything from sales and marketing to customer service and supply chain management.

One of the biggest mistakes companies make is assuming that just because a process works at a small scale, it will work on a larger one. However, processes that are too dependent on specific individuals, lack automation or rely on informal communication methods can quickly become bottlenecks when the organization grows. Strengthening core operations requires streamlining workflows, reducing inefficiencies, and ensuring every department can function autonomously without constant oversight.

Automation is also critical in this phase. Businesses should invest in technology and software that can help standardize repetitive tasks, minimize human error, and improve efficiency. From CRM systems that manage customer interactions to financial software that ensures real-time cash flow tracking, scalable operations rely on technology to create consistency and predictability. Strengthening core operations isn't about making work more complex—it's about creating simplicity and efficiency to sustain growth.

TEST THE CULTURE UNDER PRESSURE

Culture isn't just about creating a positive work environment—it's the invisible force that holds a company together during rapid growth. A business with a weak culture will struggle when new challenges arise, employees feel overwhelmed, or new team members don't align with the company's values. Leaders must proactively test their organizational culture before scaling to ensure it can withstand the pressures of growth.

One effective way to do this is by intentionally introducing controlled stress into the organization. This could take the form of simulated high-pressure scenarios, crisis management exercises, or temporarily restructuring certain roles to gauge how teams adapt to change. The goal is to observe how employees respond to uncertainty and whether the company's values hold firm under pressure. Do employees collaborate effectively under stress, or do silos and blame-shifting emerge? Do leaders maintain composure and decisiveness or falter when the stakes are raised?

Another key consideration is whether the company has a clearly defined culture that can be maintained as it grows. If a business scales too quickly without reinforcing its core values, it risks losing the essence of what made it successful in the first place. Hiring at scale also presents a cultural risk—bringing in too many new employees too quickly can dilute the company's identity if there's no structured onboarding process in place to reinforce core values. Culture must be deliberately cultivated and reinforced, or it will erode under the weight of expansion.

EVALUATE FINANCIAL RESILIENCE

One of the most dangerous myths in business is that scaling automatically leads to higher profits. While growth is often associated with financial success, the reality is that scaling requires significant upfront investment, and many businesses run into serious financial trouble when they attempt to grow without a solid financial foundation.

A thorough financial audit is essential before scaling. Leaders must analyze their cash flow, burn rate, and capital reserves to determine whether the business can sustain the increased expenses that come with expansion. Payroll costs will rise, operational expenses will increase, and infrastructure investments will be necessary. If a business already operates on thin margins, attempting to scale prematurely can quickly lead to financial strain.

In addition to analyzing current financial health, companies must also forecast different scaling scenarios. What happens if revenue growth slows while expenses increase? How much capital is needed to sustain operations during a transition period? Will outside funding be necessary, and how will it impact ownership and decision-making? Businesses that scale smartly take a data-driven approach to financial planning, ensuring that they have the financial resilience to weather both the opportunities and the risks of growth.

IDENTIFY THE RIGHT LEADERSHIP FOR THE NEXT STAGE

Leadership is one of the most overlooked factors in scaling. Many companies assume that the same leadership team that successfully managed the business in its early stages will be equally effective at a larger scale. However, scaling a business requires different skill sets, mindsets, and decision-making abilities than running a smaller operation. I cannot emphasize this enough. It's very important.

The transition from a small company to a larger organization often exposes gaps in leadership capabilities. Leaders who thrive in a hands-on, entrepreneurial environment may struggle with a growing company's more structured, strategic demands. Decision-making processes must shift from instinct-driven to data-driven. Leaders must also learn to delegate more effectively, trusting their teams to execute without micromanagement.

Another critical aspect of pre-scale leadership assessment is identifying gaps in expertise. Scaling often requires bringing in new leadership talent with experience in areas that may not have been a priority in the past. For example, a company that previously relied on a generalist operations manager may need a dedicated supply chain expert. A founder who led the sales efforts early on may need to step back and hire a VP of Sales to take the business to the next level. Leadership must evolve in alignment with the company's growth trajectory.

Investing in leadership development before scaling can prevent significant growing pains. Executive coaching, mentorship programs, and strategic hiring can help ensure the leadership team is equipped to successfully navigate the complexities of scaling.

BUILD SCALABILITY INTO EVERY SYSTEM

One of the most common reasons companies struggle when scaling is that their systems were never designed to handle increased demand. Businesses that successfully scale don't just grow their customer base or expand their workforce—they build systems that can support long-term, sustainable growth.

A fundamental question every leader must ask before scaling is: If the company doubled in size tomorrow, could its current systems handle the increased demand? If the answer is no, then scaling prematurely will create operational chaos.

Scalable systems include everything from technology infrastructure to customer experience frameworks. A business that relies on manual processes for order fulfillment, customer service, or data tracking will struggle to maintain quality as volume increases. Investing in scalable technology—such as automated workflow tools, cloud-based data management systems, and AI-driven customer support—ensures the company can handle growth without compromising efficiency.

Scalability also applies to people and organizational structure. If scaling requires hiring dozens or even hundreds of new employees, is a clear onboarding and training process in place? Can the company's management structure adapt to oversee a larger workforce without becoming bureaucratic and slow? Building scalability into every system ensures that growth doesn't come at the expense of operational effectiveness.

SCALING SMART: THE PRE-SCALE IMPERATIVE

So, scaling a business isn't about chasing growth at all costs—it's about ensuring that every aspect of the organization is prepared for the increased demands that come with expansion. Strengthening core operations, stress-testing company culture, evaluating financial resilience, refining leadership capabilities, and building scalable systems are all pre-scale processes.

Businesses that skip this critical phase often find themselves struggling to manage the chaos that comes with rapid expansion. However, companies that take the time to prepare before scaling set themselves up for sustainable, long-term success. Scaling isn't just about doing more—it's about doing better to ensure the organization thrives, no matter how large it grows.

This was something I had seen go wrong in high-stakes investigations. In cases where cyber intrusions escalated rapidly, agencies that didn't have scalable response systems in place found themselves over-whelmed and ineffective. The same applies to business. If your infrastructure can't scale, neither can your success.

SCALING IS EARNED, NOT ASSUMED

Leaders' biggest mistake is assuming they're ready to scale simply because they've had initial success. Early wins can be deceptive, creating the illusion that momentum alone will carry a business through the next stage of growth. However, momentum without a solid foundation can just as easily lead to disaster. Scaling isn't a reward for getting through the launch phase—it's a responsibility that must be earned through careful preparation, deliberate strategy, and discipline to ensure sustainable growth. Too many businesses fail not because they didn't have a good product or service but because they scale prematurely without securing the operational, cultural, and financial structures necessary to support long-term expansion.

Leaders often get caught up in the allure of rapid growth, believing that if demand exists, the organization must immediately capitalize on it. However, real success isn't measured by how quickly a company can grow but by how well that growth can be managed without compromising efficiency, quality, or long-term stability. Scaling requires more than just hiring more people, selling more products, or expanding into new markets. It demands a transformation in how an organization operates, its leaders make decisions, and how its culture withstands the stress of change. A business not built for scalability will start to crack under pressure as it expands—customer service will falter, operations will slow down, and leadership will struggle to maintain control. Pay attention to the details!

Business leaders often glorify growth, but the true measure of success isn't just expansion—it's endurance. A company that scales too soon will struggle to survive, often burning through resources, overwhelming its teams, and eroding the quality of its offerings. But a company that scales smartly will thrive for the long haul. It will grow at a pace that ensures long-term stability, not short-term wins. It will build a reputation not just for its ability to expand but for its ability to maintain excellence as it does so. It will be resilient in the face of change and prepared for the challenges that come with scaling rather than scrambling to keep up.

Pre-scale isn't a delay. It's the difference between building something that lasts and something that collapses under its weight. It's the difference between chasing growth and managing it wisely. It's the difference between reacting to opportunities and being prepared for them. Leaders who understand this distinction are the ones who build companies that stand the test of time. Those who ignore it often struggle to keep their businesses from unraveling when they grow too fast or too soon.

In the next chapter, we'll dive into the first major shift leaders must make when transitioning from stability to scale: defining a scalable vision and aligning the entire organization around it. Without a clear, unified vision, even the best-laid growth plans can falter. We'll explore how leaders can create a strategic roadmap for expansion, ensuring that every team member is aligned with the company's long-term objectives and that scaling efforts are driven by purpose, not just ambition. Then, we'll dive into the principles every leader needs to scale.

2

SCALING YOUR VISION BEFORE SCALING YOUR COMPANY

Scaling a business isn't just about increasing revenue, hiring more people, or expanding into new markets. At its core, scaling is about clarity—defining a scalable vision that aligns the entire organization toward a common goal. Without this alignment, even the most well-intentioned growth efforts can lead to disorganization, inefficiency, and failure. The companies that scale successfully aren't just those that grow fast but those that grow with purpose, ensuring every decision and initiative serves a greater, long-term mission. This chapter explores why defining a scalable vision is the first and most critical step in any growth strategy and how leaders can create one that ensures alignment, efficiency, and long-term success.

THE ILLUSION OF VISION

Many leaders assume they have a vision simply because they have goals. However, a vision is not a revenue target, a market expansion plan, or an ambitious hiring strategy. A vision is an overarching, unifying idea that is the foundation for everything a company does. Without it, businesses may achieve growth but struggle to sustain it because their efforts are scattered and reactive instead of focused and intentional.

Borders Group is a notable example of a major U.S. corporation that suffered from an illusion of its vision. Founded in 1971, Borders became a prominent international book and music retailer. The company's vision centered on providing an extensive in-store selection of books and media. However, as consumer preferences shifted towards online shopping and digital media, Borders was slow to adapt. The company underestimated the impact of e-commerce and digital reading devices, leading to its inability to compete effectively in the evolving market. Without embracing technological advancements, this steadfast adherence to its traditional business model ultimately led to Borders filing for bankruptcy in 2011.

Another example is Nokia, once a global leader in mobile phone manufacturing. In the early 2000s, Nokia's vision was focused on producing high-quality hardware for mobile devices. However, the company failed to anticipate the rapid shift towards smartphones with advanced operating systems and app ecosystems. Nokia's reluctance to innovate and adapt its vision to the changing technological landscape allowed competitors like Apple and Samsung to capture significant market share. This misalignment between Nokia's vision and the industry's direction contributed to its decline in the mobile phone market.

These cases illustrate the dangers of companies becoming enamored with their initial visions, leading to a lack of adaptability in the face of industry transformations. Such an illusion of vision can result in missed opportunities and business failure.

When I stepped into my role in the private sector, I also initially believed that our path to scaling was straightforward. The company where I served as CEO had a strong product, a talented team, and growing demand. But what became clear quickly was that while we had ambitions, we lacked alignment. Each department had its own interpretation of what growth meant. Sales were focused on closing as many deals as possible, operations were concerned about keeping up with demand, and leadership was trying to balance expansion with efficiency. Without a unifying scalable vision, our growth was chaotic rather than strategic.

CREATING A SCALABLE VISION

So, how do leaders define a vision that doesn't sound inspiring on paper but supports scalable, long-term growth? Three key elements must be present:

IT MUST BE CLEAR AND ACTIONABLE

A vision is only effective if it is clearly understood at every level of the organization. A vague mission statement like "We aim to be the best in our industry" is meaningless if employees don't know how that translates into daily decisions and actions. A scalable vision must be specific enough to provide clear direction while remaining flexible enough to evolve as the company grows.

When I served as CEO, once we recognized the need for a clearer vision, we rewrote our mission statement to focus on **scalable solutions that evolve with our clients' needs.** This wasn't just a tagline—it was a strategic shift that influenced everything from how we designed our products to how we trained our sales team. Every employee, from engineers to account managers, understood that our goal wasn't just to sell more and provide solutions that could grow with the businesses we served. That level of clarity transformed the way we operated.

The United States Intelligence Community (USIC), in its post-9/11 transformation, also had to make its vision crystal clear: **Prevent terrorism through intelligence-driven operations.** That wasn't just an abstract idea—it required structural changes, resource allocation shifts, and new training protocols. This meant that field agents, analysts, linguists, and others, needed to think proactively rather than reactively, that analysts had to work more closely with operational teams, and that collaboration across agencies had become a top priority. The clarity of that vision allowed the USIC to scale its capabilities without losing focus on its core mission.

IT MUST BE EMBEDDED IN DECISION-MAKING

A vision isn't something that gets written in a company handbook and forgotten. It must guide every major decision, from hiring and product development to partnerships and investments. When leaders make choices that align with the vision, employees see consistency and trust in the company's direction. When decisions conflict with the stated vision, confusion and misalignment follow.

Embedding our vision into decision-making meant prioritizing scalable technology and business practices over short-term profits. Sometimes, there were opportunities to close big deals, but we walked away if those deals required customized solutions that wouldn't scale. That was a difficult choice in the short term but crucial for our long-term growth strategy.

The USIC had to make similar decisions in prioritizing counterterrorism efforts. Before the shift in vision, resources were often allocated based on the most high-profile cases. But as the government embraced its new counterterrorism-first approach, it began investing heavily in intelligence analysis, surveillance, and proactive threat detection rather than simply reacting to crimes after they happened. That shift in resource allocation allowed the USIC to scale its effectiveness dramatically, preventing attacks rather than just investigating them.

IT MUST BE COMMUNICATED CONSTANTLY

Even the best vision is useless if it isn't consistently reinforced. Leaders must communicate it at every level—through company meetings, training programs, and performance evaluations. Employees must hear it so frequently that it becomes second nature in their decision-making. This can be hard but it's important to stay focused on this.

You should reinforced your vision in every leadership meeting and department strategy session and integrate it into your hiring process, ensuring new employees understood and aligned with our long-term mission before joining the company. The more you communicate it, the more it becomes part of your company's DNA.

The USIC also learned this lesson during its restructuring. Initially, not all personnel understood or accepted the new counterterrorism-first approach. To address this, leadership within various agencies implemented ongoing training programs, embedded intelligence-driven priorities into every field office. It required every division to align its work with the broader mission. The result was a cultural shift that allowed scaling efforts to succeed.

SCALING WITH PURPOSE

Defining a scalable vision isn't about crafting an inspirational slogan—it's about creating a unifying force that directs every aspect of a company's growth. Leaders who fail to establish this clarity before scaling often deal with operational chaos, cultural disconnection, and inconsistent decision-making. But those who invest the time in getting this right set their organizations up for long-term success. Invest the time!

In the next chapter, we'll dive into how leaders can structure their organizations for scalability, ensuring that their teams, processes, and systems are designed to support sustained growth rather than collapse under its weight.

Now, let's dive into the 10 principles every leader needs to master before scaling. These principles aren't just theoretical concepts; they are the foundation for sustainable growth. Without them, scaling becomes a chaotic and overwhelming process, filled with misalignment, inefficiencies, and leadership struggles. But when fully embraced, these principles provide a clear roadmap for navigating the complexities of expansion with confidence and control. These principles separate leaders who grow a business from those who build a lasting, scalable enterprise. They will challenge you to refine your leadership approach, rethink your strategies, and cultivate the kind of resilience and adaptability that true scaling demands. Mastering these principles will not only help you grow your organization, it will also ensure that your leadership remains strong, your culture stays intact, and your team thrives under expansion pressures. Let's get started.

3

THE LEADERSHIP BLIND SPOT –
LEARNING HOW TO LISTEN

The importance of listening to clients in business cannot be overstated. Yet, repeatedly, I see people failing to do it. Leaders must continually reinforce the value of listening within every level of their organization because it fundamentally changes the outcome of client interactions. It's not just about hearing words—it's about understanding needs, recognizing pain points, and genuinely grasping what a client's business is all about. Before a leader, a salesperson, or anyone in a client-facing role even begins to speak, they must first listen. That's the foundation of trust. And trust, in business, is everything.

Too often, I've walked into boardrooms only to be met with an endless monologue from a salesperson rattling off a rehearsed pitch. It's almost impressive how long they can talk without taking a breath, but I'm not impressed—I'm disengaged. It's clear they aren't interested in my business, my needs, or my challenges. They are just running through a scripted presentation they've probably delivered a thousand times before, and none of it resonates because they haven't taken a moment to listen.

Clients, like anyone, want to feel heard. When they do, trust develops naturally. And trust is the foundation of long-term relationships—the kind of relationships that don't just generate a single sale but evolve into valuable, enduring partnerships. I've seen it happen repeatedly: businesses prioritizing listening don't just win clients; they build loyalty, credibility, and long-term success. When clients know they are truly understood, they are far more likely to engage, collaborate, and invest in a lasting business relationship.

Indeed, scaling a business is impossible without mastering the art of listening. Growth doesn't just require strategy, capital, or vision—it requires a deep understanding of people. Leaders who don't listen fail to grasp their employees' concerns, customers' needs, and the shifts in their industry. Without this awareness, attempts to scale are built on a shaky foundation, increasing the risk of operational breakdowns, cultural disconnect, and strategic missteps. The ability to listen isn't just a leadership skill; it's a survival skill for any organization looking to expand. In this chapter, we explore why listening is often the missing piece in leadership and how failing to listen can stall, or even reverse, the trajectory of a growing business.

Most leadership books and business conferences focus on the importance of communication—how to inspire, how to persuade, and how to articulate a vision. But rarely do they emphasize the most critical, yet often overlooked, component of effective leadership: listening. Leaders pride themselves on decisiveness, confidence, and vision, yet these qualities can make them deaf to the people they serve. True leadership is not just about being heard; it's about hearing others. Most people if asked will tell you "I'm a good listener." In reality, I have seen very few listen well.

WHY LEADERS DON'T LISTEN

Leaders, by nature, are problem solvers. They are conditioned to act, make decisions, and move things forward. On the other hand, listening is often perceived as passive—a delay in action rather than an essential part. In fast-paced environments, where time is a currency, leaders may unconsciously de-prioritize listening in favor of making quick calls based on their own instincts and experience.

Another reason leaders don't listen enough is ego. Successful individuals often reach leadership positions because they are confident in their decisions, ambitious in their pursuits, and able to push through obstacles with the sheer force of will. While these traits help in rising to the top, they can become blind spots when it comes to leading effectively. If leaders believe they already have the right answers, they will see little value in pausing to gather input from others.

Additionally, organizational structures can discourage listening. In hierarchical settings, employees are often hesitant to speak up, particularly when their perspectives challenge the opinions of those in power. This creates an echo chamber where leaders hear only what they want to hear, further reinforcing their belief that their approach is correct. When subordinates feel their voices don't matter, they stop offering valuable insights, leaving leaders with an incomplete picture of reality. You'll run your company into an iceberg if you allow this to occur.

THE COST OF NOT LISTENING

The failure to listen comes at a steep price. Leaders who do not actively seek input, ask the right questions, and create an environment where others feel heard will inevitably make decisions based on flawed or incomplete information. The consequences of poor listening can manifest in multiple ways

One of the most valuable lessons I have learned from listening to clients over the years is the ability to truly understand their needs. By actively engaging with clients and hearing what they are saying—beyond just their words—businesses can gain deeper insights into their expectations, preferences, and challenges. This understanding allows companies to tailor their products and services to meet client needs better, leading to higher satisfaction, stronger loyalty, and long-term partnerships. The businesses that thrive are the ones that prioritize listening as a core function, not just a passive activity.

LOSS OF INNOVATION

When employees feel unheard, they stop contributing ideas—not out of a lack of creativity, but because they perceive that their insights won't be valued or acted upon. Many of the most successful companies thrive because their leaders embrace diverse perspectives, foster a psychologically safe environment, and encourage open dialogue. However, when a leader dismisses feedback or operates with a top-down approach, employees quickly learn that innovation is neither expected nor rewarded.

In such environments, individuals shift from being proactive problem-solvers to passive task-doers, merely following instructions rather than challenging norms or seeking improvements. This kills creative momentum and discourages risk-taking, two essential components of progress. Over time, a company that fails to innovate is stagnating, unable to evolve alongside changing market demands or emerging technologies. Competitors who do embrace a culture of listening and innovation will quickly outpace them, making their business model obsolete. The loss of innovation isn't immediate—a slow deterioration that eventually makes the company irrelevant.

LOW MORALE AND HIGH TURNOVER

When employees do not feel heard, they feel undervalued, directly impacting their motivation, job satisfaction, and commitment to the organization. Studies have consistently shown that one of the top reasons people leave their jobs is not due to compensation but rather a lack of recognition, respect, and the feeling that their voice matters. When leaders don't listen, employees disengage, leading to decreased productivity, lower quality work, and higher turnover rates.

High-performing individuals, in particular, will not stay in environments where their contributions are ignored. These employees drive growth, push boundaries, and bring fresh perspectives—yet they are also the most likely to leave if they feel unheard. The departure of such employees creates a ripple effect within the organization. Not only does it result in a loss of valuable talent, but it also negatively impacts team morale. Remaining employees start questioning whether they too, should look elsewhere for an environment where their ideas and concerns are taken seriously.

Additionally, high turnover is costly. The expense of recruiting, hiring, and training new employees is substantial, and when turnover becomes excessive, it disrupts workflow, damages team cohesion, and can negatively impact company culture. Leaders who fail to listen may find themselves caught in an endless cycle of hiring and replacing talent without ever addressing the root cause of the problem. I have seen this many times in both small and big companies.

POOR DECISION-MAKING

Decisions made in isolation, without input from those on the front lines, often lead to poor outcomes. Leaders who surround themselves with "yes men" and fail to engage in active listening create a dangerous echo chamber where only reinforcing opinions are heard rather than a range of insights and potential concerns. In these environments, critical warning signs are ignored, risks are underestimated, and the organization becomes blind to its own weaknesses.

Good decision-making requires diverse perspectives, constructive debate, and a willingness to challenge assumptions. Leaders who refuse to listen to those closest to the day-to-day operations—whether that be employees, customers, or advisors—often make strategic errors that could have been avoided had they sought broader input. These errors might include launching a product that doesn't meet market needs, failing to address internal inefficiencies, or making financial investments that backfire due to unforeseen complications.

Poor listening also contributes to reactionary decision-making. Instead of anticipating and proactively addressing challenges, leaders who don't listen constantly play defense, scrambling to fix problems that could have been avoided with the right insights at the right time. A business that makes consistently poor decisions due to a lack of listening ultimately loses its competitive edge, alienates its workforce, and erodes stakeholder trust.

CUSTOMER DISCONNECT

In business, failing to listen doesn't just affect employees—it also alienates customers. Organizations that don't listen to their clients' needs, preferences, or complaints eventually lose their market relevance. Many businesses that once dominated their industries—such as Kodak, Blockbuster, and Nokia—failed to adapt because their leaders ignored key signals from customers about shifting preferences and emerging trends.

Customers are the lifeblood of any business, and their needs constantly evolve. Companies that listen actively—through customer feedback, data analytics, and direct engagement—can adjust their strategies, improve their offerings, and maintain customer loyalty. Conversely, businesses that operate under the assumption that they know best are doomed to fail without listening to their market. If you don't trust me on this, try asking your team, "what did you hear?" after your next meeting. You might be surprised by what you hear!

For instance, when Netflix introduced streaming, Blockbuster had every opportunity to adapt and compete. However, its leadership remained committed to its outdated business model, ignoring customer frustrations with late fees and the growing demand for digital convenience. By the time Blockbuster attempted to pivot, it was too late—Netflix had already cemented its dominance.

Similarly, companies that ignore customer complaints about product quality, service experience, or pricing strategies will lose ground to competitors actively listening and responding. Customer disconnect leads to declining sales, damaged brand reputation, and business failure.

CRISIS AMPLIFICATION

Ignoring employee concerns, customer complaints, or internal conflicts allows small problems to fester into major crises. Leaders who dismiss early warning signs because they are unwilling to listen often deal with full-scale disasters that could have been mitigated or prevented entirely.

A lack of listening can turn minor grievances into widespread dissatisfaction, workplace conflicts into toxic cultures, and operational inefficiencies into catastrophic failures. For example, when employees repeatedly voice concerns about unethical behavior, safety risks, or poor management practices but are ignored, those issues do not disappear—they escalate. The company may eventually face legal consequences, financial losses, or severe reputational damage.

Failing to listen to complaints in customer-facing industries can lead to public relations disasters. A single unresolved customer issue can snowball into a viral scandal in today's social media-driven world. Businesses that refuse to listen and adapt often find themselves in damage-control mode, reacting to crises rather than preventing them.

Beyond the immediate business impact, crisis amplification also affects long-term trust. Employees who witness leaders dismiss concerns will hesitate to speak up in the future, fostering a culture of silence and compliance rather than one of transparency and accountability. Customers who feel ignored will take their business elsewhere and share their negative experiences with others, further damaging the company's reputation.

Listening isn't just about avoiding major crises—it's about proactively identifying small issues before they spiral out of control. A leader who listens well builds a resilient organization that is adaptable, trusted, and prepared for the inevitable challenges of growth.

History is filled with examples of executives and decision-makers who suffered major setbacks—not because they lacked intelligence or ambition, but because they refused to listen to the right people at the right time. Whether it's resisting internal pushback, disregarding customer complaints, or overlooking clear warning signs, the consequences of poor listening can be disastrous. The following examples highlight leaders who paid a steep price for their failure to listen, demonstrating how a lack of attentiveness can lead to financial ruin, reputational damage, and even legal consequences.

As CEO of Hewlett-Packard (HP), Carly Fiorina, from 1999 to 2005, spearheaded the controversial merger with Compaq in 2001. Despite strong opposition from board members, notably Walter Hewlett, son of HP's co-founder, Fiorina pushed forward with the $25 billion acquisition. Critics argued that she did not adequately heed concerns about the merger's potential risks and the cultural integration challenges between the two companies. The aftermath saw HP's stock price drop by 50%, and the anticipated benefits of the merger did not materialize as expected. This period was marked by internal discord and strategic missteps, leading to Fiorina's forced resignation in 2005.

Paula Vennells, CEO of the UK's Post Office from 2012 to 2019, oversaw the organization during the Horizon IT scandal. The Horizon computer system, introduced in the early 2000s, was flawed, leading to financial discrepancies that falsely implicated over 4,000 sub-postmasters in theft and fraud. Despite mounting evidence and persistent complaints from sub-postmasters about system errors, Vennells and the Post Office leadership failed to listen and address these concerns adequately. This oversight resulted in wrongful prosecutions, severe personal and financial hardships for the affected individuals, and a significant miscarriage of justice. The scandal eventually led to public inquiries, legal battles, and Vennells' resignation amid intense scrutiny.

Robert Rubin, a former U.S. Treasury Secretary, joined Citigroup in 1999 and served as a director and senior advisor. During his tenure, he advocated for and oversaw strategies that involved high-risk investments and significant exposure to mortgage-backed securities. Despite internal warnings and growing concerns about the escalating risks, Rubin and other senior executives did not sufficiently heed these cautions. They didn't listen. This lack of attentiveness contributed to Citigroup's substantial losses during the 2008 financial crisis, leading to a $45 billion federal bailout through the Troubled Asset Relief Program (TARP). Rubin resigned from his position in 2009, facing criticism for his role in the company's financial troubles and for not adequately addressing the risks that led to the crisis.

These examples underscore the critical importance of leaders actively listening to internal and external voices. Ignoring or dismissing concerns can lead to strategic errors, financial losses, and damage to an organization's reputation. It's dangerous to think you're the smartest person in the room. You may be right nine times out of ten, but not always!

THE ART OF LISTENING AS A LEADERSHIP SKILL

Listening isn't just about hearing—it's about improving. When businesses take the time to listen to their clients, they can identify pain points and areas for improvement within the customer experience.

Every client interaction with a company should be seamless and productive, but that doesn't happen by accident. It happens when businesses intentionally gather feedback, address concerns, and make strategic adjustments based on what they hear. Enhancing the customer experience begins with understanding exactly where friction points exist and eliminating them.

True client engagement requires more than just a transactional relationship; it necessitates a valuable feedback loop that benefits both the client and the business. By actively listening to their ideas, concerns, and frustrations, companies can drive meaningful innovation—creating new products, refining services, and staying ahead of changing market demands. The reality is, the business landscape is constantly shifting, and the companies that fail to listen are the ones that fall behind. We saw this play out dramatically in the aftermath of COVID-19, where companies that adapted to customer needs survived, while those that ignored them struggled or disappeared. The real value lies in becoming a true client partner, not just another vendor.

The good news is that listening is a skill that can be developed. It is not merely about being quiet while others speak—it requires an intentional shift in approach, mindset, and practice.

CULTIVATE ACTIVE LISTENING

Active listening means fully engaging with the person speaking rather than thinking about how to respond or waiting for them to finish. This requires eye contact, body language that signals attentiveness, and paraphrasing key points to ensure understanding. It also means being present—physically and mentally— by eliminating distractions and focusing entirely on the speaker. Leaders who master active listening gain deeper insights and build stronger relationships, as people feel genuinely heard and understood.

ASK OPEN-ENDED QUESTIONS

Instead of assuming you know what people need, ask open-ended questions, encouraging them to share more. Questions like *"What challenges are you facing?"* or *"How would you improve this process?"* invite deeper discussions and uncover insights that may have otherwise remained hidden. How leaders frame their questions can determine whether they receive a surface-level answer or a meaningful, constructive response. Open-ended questions foster creativity, encourage problem-solving, and often lead to solutions that would not have surfaced through directives or leading inquiries.

CREATE A SAFE SPACE FOR FEEDBACK

Leaders must actively create an environment where employees feel comfortable speaking up. This means not just inviting feedback but demonstrating that it is valued. Leaders should respond with curiosity rather than defensiveness when someone offers a critique or suggestion. A culture of psychological safety allows employees to voice concerns without fear of judgment or retaliation, leading to a more transparent, innovative, and engaged workplace. People who believe their opinions matter become more invested in the organization's success, fostering collaboration and trust across teams.

LISTEN TO WHAT'S NOT BEING SAID

Some of the most important insights come from what people don't say. Pay attention to hesitation, tone, and body language. If employees are quiet in meetings but vocal in private conversations, it may indicate an issue with trust or company culture. Leaders should also take note of patterns—if the same issues keep arising through indirect channels rather than direct communication, it may signal deeper organizational problems. Being attuned to these subtle cues helps leaders address concerns before they escalate, creating a work environment where honesty and openness are encouraged.

HOW LAW ENFORCEMENT TAUGHT ME TO LISTEN

My years in law enforcement provided an unexpected but invaluable lesson in listening. In high-pressure situations, where people are under stress or in crisis, truly hearing what someone is saying (and what they aren't saying) is critical. I quickly learned that effective policing wasn't just about authority and understanding people's motivations, fears, and intentions. For example, a suspect in an interrogation often reveals more through body language and tone than through their words. Witnesses withholding information might not lie outright, but their hesitations, evasions, and discomfort often provide crucial clues. Learning to listen in these moments wasn't just a tactical skill—it was the difference between solving a case and missing a critical detail.

This experience shaped the way I approach leadership in business. Running a company isn't all that different from leading an investigation. Employees, clients, and partners all have motivations, frustrations, and aspirations that they may not verbalize outright. A leader who listens intently, reads between the lines, and creates an environment where people feel safe speaking the truth will always have an advantage.

The best decisions I've made in business have come from listening to the people around me. Whether it was an employee raising a concern I hadn't considered, a client hinting at an emerging trend, or a mentor providing tough feedback, the times I truly opened my ears and absorbed what was being said were the times I gained the most valuable insights.

THE LEADERSHIP EVOLUTION: FROM TALKING TO LISTENING

Many leaders assume their primary role is to provide direction, make decisions, and drive execution. While those elements are important, the most impactful leaders understand that their greatest responsibility is not to talk but to listen. Listening is what turns a manager into a leader, an organization into a community, and a business into an enduring success.

Leaders who listen build stronger teams, make better decisions and create environments where people thrive. They are not just problem solvers—they are problem preventers. They are not just strategists— they are human connectors. And they are not just decision-makers—they are the kind of leaders people want to follow.

In the next chapter, we will explore how listening is not just about hearing words—it's about translating what you learn into action. Because listening, on its own, is not enough. The true power of listening comes from what you do with the knowledge it provides.

4

PROVIDING VALUE – THE TRUE MEASURE OF SCALING SUCCESS

Scaling isn't about growth for growth's sake. It's not just about increasing revenue, expanding market share, or hiring more employees. While these are often the metrics businesses focus on, true, sustainable expansion happens when an organization consistently delivers value. Without this foundation, growth is hollow—an illusion of success that eventually collapses under its own weight.

Businesses that scale smartly don't measure success solely by their ability to get bigger; they focus on enhancing customer experience, improving their products or services, and maintaining relevance in their industry. The organizations that thrive long-term aren't those that grow the fastest but those that grow with purpose. This chapter explores why delivering value is the foundation of successful scaling, the pitfalls of chasing growth without substance, and how leaders can ensure their organizations remain valuable even as they expand.

In today's fast-moving business environment, providing value as a leader requires a combination of traditional leadership principles and modern, adaptive strategies. One of the most critical aspects of leadership today is fostering a culture built on trust, inclusivity, and diversity. Organizations struggle to innovate, retain talent, and maintain a competitive edge without these foundational elements.

A leader's ability to establish trust and make every team member feel valued is what ultimately drives performance. People do their best work when they feel heard and respected, regardless of their background or role. When leaders actively promote inclusivity, they unlock the full potential of their teams, encouraging diverse perspectives that lead to more creative and effective solutions. Innovation doesn't happen in environments where employees feel dismissed or overlooked—it happens in workplaces where they know their contributions matter.

Business moves faster than ever, and leaders must cultivate teams that don't just keep up but stay ahead of the market. The ability to anticipate shifts, adapt strategies, and proactively innovate is what separates high-performing organizations from those that fall behind.

However, no team will consistently think ahead or take risks if they don't feel valued by leadership. A leader who listens, empowers, and supports their team creates an environment where forward-thinking ideas thrive and business success follows. This literally can make or break a company. It's that important.

WHY VALUE MATTERS MORE
THAN GROWTH

Growth without value is a recipe for disaster. Many companies prioritize rapid expansion without ensuring that their products, services, and customer relationships can sustain that growth. This is often fueled by the pressure to meet investor expectations, increase quarterly profits, or outpace competitors. However, scaling too fast without a strong foundation of value can lead to operational breakdowns, customer dissatisfaction, and, ultimately, decline.

Consider some of the most notorious business failures. Companies like WeWork, Theranos, and Pets.com expanded aggressively but failed because they didn't create lasting value. They built businesses based on hype, inflated valuations, and unsustainable promises rather than focusing on solving real problems and delivering meaningful benefits to their customers.

True scaling is about **adding capacity while preserving and enhancing value**. The companies that stand the test of time—Apple or Amazon, to name two—have scaled not by merely growing but by continually increasing the value they provide to customers. They invest in innovation, customer experience, and long-term strategy rather than chasing short-term metrics.

THE PITFALLS OF GROWTH FOR GROWTH'S SAKE

Many organizations mistakenly believe that scaling is simply about doing more—more revenue, more customers, more locations. However, without a deliberate focus on delivering value, growth becomes unsustainable and can lead to a range of challenges that threaten long-term success.

When companies scale too quickly without maintaining service quality, customer satisfaction suffers. A rapid influx of demand can overwhelm customer support teams, create inconsistencies in product quality, and lead to logistical failures. What was once a trusted brand with a loyal customer base can quickly become known for poor service, delayed deliveries, or subpar experiences. When customer expectations are no longer met, loyalty erodes, and competitors who maintain high standards step in to take their place.

Unchecked growth also puts a significant strain on internal operations. Expanding too fast stretches processes, teams, and infrastructure beyond their limits, leading to inefficiencies and costly mistakes. Many startups that grow at an unsustainable pace find themselves unable to meet demand, causing delayed orders, inventory mismanagement, and employee burnout. Without a solid operational foundation, what may seem like an exciting opportunity for expansion can quickly spiral into logistical chaos.

Financial instability is another major consequence of uncontrolled growth. Companies often pour resources into expansion efforts—hiring more employees, opening new locations, and launching aggressive marketing campaigns—without ensuring their revenue streams and profit margins can sustain these expenditures. Leadership may assume that increased size will automatically lead to profitability, but rapid scaling can result in mounting debt, forced downsizing, or even business failure without careful financial management.

Scaling too fast can also erode company culture and identity. Employees who once felt deeply connected to the organization's mission may struggle to adapt to rapid changes in structure, priorities, and leadership styles. As growth takes precedence over maintaining core values, company culture weakens, leading to disengagement, high turnover, and a decline in overall performance. Once focused on the vision and purpose of the company, leadership may become consumed with expansion metrics, losing sight of the foundation that made the organization successful in the first place.

HOW TO SCALE BY PROVIDING VALUE

The best companies scale **because** they deliver value—not in spite of it. Here's how leaders can ensure that they continue to prioritize value creation as they grow.

1. FOCUS ON THE CUSTOMER EXPERIENCE

At the heart of value creation is the customer. Companies that scale successfully do so by obsessing over their customers' needs, preferences, and pain points. Amazon, for example, built its empire not by chasing revenue but by relentlessly improving customer experience—whether through fast shipping, personalized recommendations, or superior customer support.

KEY STRATEGIES TO MAINTAIN CUSTOMER EXPERIENCE WHILE SCALING:

- Implement robust feedback loops to learn from customers continuously.

- Invest in customer service teams and technology to handle increased demand.

- Ensure consistency in product and service quality, regardless of how big the company grows.

2. IMPROVE PRODUCT OR SERVICE QUALITY

Scaling isn't just about reaching more people—it's about ensuring that what you offer continues to be excellent. Companies must continuously innovate and refine their products or services as they grow. You need to look out in front of the car when you drive! It's the same thing in business!

WAYS TO MAINTAIN PRODUCT EXCELLENCE DURING SCALING:

- Invest in research and development to stay ahead of industry trends.

- Establish strong quality control measures.

- Regularly test and improve offerings based on customer feedback.

3. STRENGTHEN YOUR INFRASTRUCTURE

A strong operational backbone is essential for scaling successfully. This includes technology, processes, and talent. Without these in place, growth becomes chaotic rather than strategic.

STEPS TO BUILD SCALABLE INFRASTRUCTURE:

- Automate repetitive tasks to improve efficiency.

- Hire and train employees who align with the company's mission.

- Implement scalable technology systems that can grow with the company.

4. MAINTAIN FINANCIAL DISCIPLINE

Expanding recklessly can lead to financial trouble. Smart scaling requires careful financial planning to ensure that growth is sustainable.

HOW TO MAINTAIN FINANCIAL HEALTH WHILE SCALING:

- Focus on profitability, not just revenue.

- Monitor key financial metrics like cash flow and gross margins.

- Avoid over-leveraging by ensuring expansion efforts are backed by real demand.

5. STAY TRUE TO YOUR MISSION AND CULTURE

One of companies' biggest mistakes when scaling is losing sight of their core mission and values. Growth should enhance culture, not erode it.

WAYS TO PRESERVE CULTURE DURING EXPANSION:

- Clearly define and communicate company values.

- Foster leadership that upholds and reinforces the company's mission.

- Ensure hiring and onboarding processes align with company culture.

COMPANIES THAT SCALED BY PROVIDING VALUE

Some of the most successful companies in the world scaled not by prioritizing growth for growth's sake but by doubling down on delivering value. These businesses understood that long-term success depends on providing exceptional customer experiences, developing superior products, and maintaining an unwavering commitment to their core mission.

APPLE: INNOVATION AND CUSTOMER LOYALTY

Apple doesn't just sell products—it creates an ecosystem of seamless, high-quality experiences. Every time Apple expands—whether launching new products or entering new markets—it focuses on customer experience, design, and functionality. The company's success in scaling is rooted in its dedication to innovation, ensuring that each product improves upon the last.

The seamless integration between Apple's hardware, software, and services creates an ecosystem that locks in customer loyalty. Apple's App Store, Apple Music, and iCloud services add value beyond just selling devices, creating long-term consumer engagement. Even as Apple scales, it strongly emphasizes user experience, consistently investing in R&D to set itself apart from competitors. Its premium pricing is justified by the level of innovation and attention to detail it delivers, ensuring that growth is always tied to delivering more value to customers.

COSTCO: PRIORITIZING VALUE OVER PROFIT MARGINS

Costco scaled successfully by maintaining its commitment to offering high-quality products at the lowest possible prices. Rather than focusing on short-term profits, it reinvested in customer benefits—leading to strong customer loyalty and sustainable growth. Unlike many retailers that chase higher margins, Costco operates on a membership-based model that allows it to pass savings directly to consumers.

Its strategy of keeping product markups low, maintaining high inventory turnover, and negotiating the best prices with suppliers ensures that customers always receive significant value. Even as it expands globally, Costco has stayed true to its core principle of delivering affordability without compromising on quality. It also invests in employee wages and benefits, recognizing that engaged and well-compensated employees contribute to a superior customer experience. This long-term commitment to value, rather than short-term profit maximization, has made Costco one of the world's most resilient and scalable retail brands.

THE LEADERSHIP MINDSET FOR VALUE-DRIVEN SCALING

Scaling successfully requires leaders to shift their mindset. Instead of asking, *"How fast can we grow?"* they should ask, *"How can we deliver even more value as we grow?"* The companies that sustain success view scaling as a **byproduct of value creation** rather than the primary goal.

By focusing on customers, maintaining quality, strengthening infrastructure, managing finances wisely, and staying true to their mission, leaders can build organizations that don't just grow but thrive. True scaling isn't about expanding as quickly as possible but growing **with purpose, intention, and value at the core.**

In the next chapter, we'll explore another critical element of leadership: knowing when to ask for help. The best leaders recognize that they can't scale alone—and the ability to seek guidance, build strong teams, and leverage expertise is essential for sustainable success.

5

I NEED HELP – THE POWER OF SEEKING SUPPORT IN SCALING SUCCESS

Time. As a leader, you never have enough of it. Feeling overwhelmed by your workload is a clear sign that something needs to change. When the volume of tasks becomes unmanageable, leaders must recognize the need for support. A CEO or executive's primary responsibility isn't to handle every detail—it's to focus on strategic decisions that drive the business forward. Let me say this again: time is one of the most valuable commodities a leader has. You need it. You need to protect it. And you need to figure out how to get more of it.

Recognizing an overwhelming workload isn't just about personal stress—it's about maintaining organizational efficiency and leadership effectiveness. One of the first warning signs is a decline in productivity. If tasks are piling up, deadlines are being missed, and decision-making feels rushed or reactive, it's a clear indication that you're stretched too thin. This can create a ripple effect throughout the organization, leading to decreased work quality, stalled momentum, and a team that is just as overwhelmed as you are.

Leaders who fail to manage their time effectively don't just burn themselves out—they weaken the entire company structure. The ability to step back, delegate, and restructure priorities isn't just a leadership skill; it's necessary for long-term success.

Scaling a business is often viewed as a leader's ability to push forward with unwavering confidence and determination. While resilience and vision are crucial, one of the most overlooked—yet most essential—qualities of a successful leader is admitting when help is needed. No leader can scale an organization alone. The myth of the self-sufficient, all-knowing executive is just that—a myth. True, sustainable growth happens when leaders recognize their limitations, seek guidance, and build a strong support system around them. Admitting that you need help—whether from mentors, advisors, or your own team—is a sign of strength, not weakness.

In this chapter, we explore why leaders who embrace collaboration, delegation, and mentorship are far more effective at scaling their businesses. We will examine the dangers of leadership isolation, the benefits of leveraging external and internal expertise, and how fostering a culture of trust and support leads to long-term growth.

THE MYTH OF THE SELF-MADE LEADER

The idea of the "self-made" leader is deeply embedded in entrepreneurial culture. Business icons are often portrayed as lone visionaries who single-handedly built their companies from the ground up. While these narratives make for compelling stories, they rarely reflect reality. Even the most successful entrepreneurs—Steve Jobs, Jeff Bezos, and others—relied on mentors, advisors, and teams to navigate challenges and accelerate their companies' growth.

Leaders who buy into the myth of self-sufficiency often resist seeking help because they fear it will make them appear weak or incompetent. This mindset stifles personal growth and hinders the organization's ability to scale. Refusing to ask for help creates bottlenecks, limits innovation, and leads to burnout. The truth is, the ability to identify areas where assistance is needed—and then actively seek that assistance—is one of the most strategic moves a leader can make.

The reluctance to ask for help can also create an unhealthy work environment where employees mirror the leader's behavior. If a CEO or founder refuses to acknowledge when they need support, it sets a precedent where employees may feel pressured to do the same, fearing that seeking help will be perceived as a weakness. Over time, this can lead to a culture of silent struggle, where challenges are left unaddressed, and productivity suffers as a result.

Furthermore, leaders who refuse to seek guidance miss out on the invaluable perspective that external voices can provide. Whether it's insights from industry veterans, constructive criticism from peers, or even employee feedback on the front lines, external input often reveals blind spots that a leader may not see on their own. Successful leaders understand that growth is a collective effort and that wisdom often comes from those who have already navigated similar challenges.

THE DANGERS OF LEADERSHIP ISOLATION

When leaders attempt to do everything on their own, they risk falling into leadership isolation. This occurs when executives become disconnected from their teams, ignore external advice, and operate within an echo chamber of their own making. The consequences of leadership isolation can devastate the leader and the organization.

Leaders who isolate themselves often develop tunnel vision, making decisions based solely on their personal perspectives rather than gathering input from those with different expertise. This can result in blind spots, missed opportunities, and costly mistakes. Furthermore, isolation increases stress and mental exhaustion, leading to poor decision-making and decreased effectiveness. Scaling a business requires leaders who are adaptable, informed, and willing to listen—not those who insist on shouldering every burden alone.

History is filled with examples of CEOs who refused to seek help, believing they could navigate challenges on their own. Whether due to arrogance, fear of appearing weak, or a deep-seated belief in their own vision, these leaders ignored valuable input from experts, advisors, and even their own teams. In many cases, this reluctance led to poor decision-making, ethical failures, and, ultimately, the downfall of their companies.

Elizabeth Holmes, the founder and former CEO of Theranos, is one of the most infamous examples of a leader who refused to seek help, even when the company faced major scientific and operational challenges. Theranos promised to revolutionize blood testing with technology that required only a few drops of blood to run hundreds of tests. However, behind the scenes, the technology was flawed and incapable of delivering accurate results.

Instead of seeking advice from experienced medical professionals, regulatory experts, or outside scientists who could have helped refine the technology or adjust business expectations, Holmes maintained a culture of secrecy. She ignored concerns from employees and outside advisors, doubling down on misleading investors and the public. Ultimately, her refusal to acknowledge the need for help resulted in Theranos' downfall, a fraud conviction, and a cautionary tale about the dangers of unchecked leadership without external accountability.

Another example is Travis Kalanick, the co-founder and former CEO of Uber, who built the company into a global giant but failed to recognize the importance of seeking help in leadership and corporate governance. Known for his aggressive, take-no-prisoners approach, Kalanick led Uber through rapid expansion but ignored calls for help addressing the company's toxic workplace culture, regulatory battles, and internal conflicts.

As reports of sexual harassment, employee mistreatment, and unethical business practices surfaced, Kalanick dismissed concerns rather than bringing in experienced HR professionals or advisors who could have helped steer the company toward a healthier, more sustainable culture. His failure to seek help from those who understood crisis management and ethical leadership eventually led to his ousting in 2017 by Uber's board, highlighting the risks of insular leadership.

Both cases illustrate how refusing to seek help—whether in navigating scientific challenges or managing corporate culture—can lead to disastrous outcomes, no matter how successful a company may appear.

THE POWER OF DELEGATION

One of the most effective ways to seek help is through delegation. Many leaders struggle with delegation because they believe no one else can execute a task as well as they can. This mindset, while understandable, often leads to burnout and limits the organization's ability to grow. A leader who insists on doing everything themselves not only overloads their own workload but also inadvertently signals to their team that they are not trusted with critical responsibilities. Over time, this creates a bottleneck in decision-making and stifles both innovation and efficiency.

While it's true that handing off responsibilities requires trust, failing to delegate is a surefire way to stunt business growth. Leaders must shift their mindset from "I can do it better" to "Someone else can do it well enough, and that's okay." Delegation is not about relinquishing control—it's about optimizing resources so that every team member operates in their zone of strength. By distributing tasks strategically, leaders free up mental bandwidth to focus on high-level strategic decisions rather than getting bogged down in day-to-day operations. The most successful companies are not built by individuals who do everything themselves but by those who empower their teams to execute effectively.

When done correctly, delegation empowers employees, enhances productivity, and creates a more agile organization. Leaders who master delegation recognize that their job is not to do everything but to ensure everything gets done by the right people. Instead of being the sole execution driver, leaders transition into facilitators, enabling their teams to take ownership of key projects. This shift increases efficiency and fosters innovation, as employees feel more confident bringing new ideas to the table when they are trusted with responsibility.

Delegation also fosters team development. Employees who are given meaningful responsibilities feel more engaged, take greater ownership of their work, and develop their leadership skills. People thrive when they are given the chance to contribute meaningfully, rather than simply executing orders. A team that is empowered to make decisions and solve problems will naturally become more invested in the company's long-term success. Additionally, delegation serves as a form of succession planning. When leaders delegate effectively, they groom future leaders within the organization who can step up and take on greater responsibilities as the company grows.

By trusting their teams, leaders cultivate a culture of accountability and continuous learning—both of which are essential for scaling a business. A company cannot scale if its growth is entirely dependent on a single person's time, energy, and decision-making capacity. Delegation allows an organization to function more independently, making it more resilient in facing challenges. Leaders who embrace delegation as a strategic tool create a more dynamic, innovative, and self-sustaining business that is not only poised for growth but also capable of thriving in the long run.

LEVERAGING MENTORS AND ADVISORS

Every great leader has had someone to guide them. Seeking mentorship is not a sign of inexperience—it is a hallmark of wisdom. Mentors provide invaluable insights, challenge assumptions, and offer a perspective that only comes with experience. A well-chosen mentor can help leaders navigate complex decisions, avoid common pitfalls, and accelerate their personal and professional growth.

Similarly, assembling a strong advisory board can give businesses strategic direction and credibility. Advisors bring specialized expertise that may not exist within the company, offering fresh perspectives on scaling challenges, financial planning, and market positioning. Leaders who tap into the knowledge and experience of mentors and advisors make more informed decisions, reducing the likelihood of costly missteps.

A strong mentor or advisor does more than just provide guidance—they hold leaders accountable. It's easy for executives to get caught up in the daily grind and lose sight of their long-term vision. A mentor or advisor serves as a trusted sounding board, offering honest feedback and constructive criticism that can help leaders stay focused on their goals. This external perspective can also challenge a leader's biases, encouraging them to consider alternative approaches and avoid falling into the trap of complacency. By regularly engaging with mentors and advisors, leaders gain the discipline and clarity needed to make strategic, well-informed decisions that drive sustainable growth.

BUILDING A LEADERSHIP TEAM YOU CAN TRUST

Scaling an organization requires leaders to surround themselves with a team of capable, trustworthy individuals. Many leaders hesitate to relinquish control, but sustainable growth depends on a leadership team that can operate independently and make critical decisions. A strong leadership team provides balance, ensuring that no single individual carries the entire weight of the company's success.

Trust is the foundation of effective leadership teams. Leaders must be willing to hire smarter, more skilled, and more experienced people in certain areas than they are. A business scales when leaders focus on what they do best and empower others to do the same. By fostering a culture of trust and collaboration, leaders create an environment where ideas flourish, innovation thrives, and the company moves forward with clarity and confidence.

A truly effective leadership team is not just a group of high-performing individuals—it is a cohesive unit that shares a common vision and works collaboratively toward achieving it. Building such a team requires clear communication, mutual respect, and a commitment to continuous development. Leaders must invest in fostering strong relationships among team members, ensuring that trust extends laterally, not just between leaders and their direct reports. When a leadership team operates with alignment and a shared sense of purpose, it creates a ripple effect throughout the entire organization, promoting efficiency, resilience, and a culture of accountability that fuels long-term success.

THE ROLE OF EMOTIONAL INTELLIGENCE IN ASKING FOR HELP

Emotional intelligence (EI) plays a crucial role in a leader's ability to seek help. Leaders with high EI are self-aware, recognize their strengths and weaknesses, and understand the importance of collaboration. The idea of seeking assistance does not threaten them; instead, they view it as an opportunity for growth. This is not discussed enough in board rooms across America.

Leaders with strong emotional intelligence also create environments where others feel comfortable offering feedback and suggestions. When employees see that their leader is open to input and willing to ask for help, they, too become more engaged in problem-solving and decision-making. This creates a culture of continuous improvement and shared accountability, where scaling becomes a collective effort rather than a solitary struggle.

Leaders with high emotional intelligence also excel at managing stress and navigating difficult situations with composure. When faced with challenges, they do not react impulsively or shut down input from others; instead, they seek diverse perspectives and carefully evaluate solutions. This ability to regulate emotions and remain open-minded fosters stronger relationships within the organization, encouraging collaboration at all levels. By demonstrating vulnerability and a willingness to learn, emotionally intelligent leaders set a powerful example—showing that true strength lies not in having all the answers but in knowing when to seek the wisdom and expertise of others.

HOW SEEKING HELP DRIVES INNOVATION

Innovation thrives in environments where collaboration is encouraged. Leaders who seek help open the door for fresh ideas, diverse perspectives, and cross-functional problem-solving. By engaging with industry experts, competitors, and even customers, leaders can uncover new opportunities for growth and adaptation.

A key indicator of an overwhelming workload is a noticeable decline in innovation and creativity within the company. When employees are stretched too thin, they become consumed with simply keeping up with daily tasks, leaving little room for strategic thinking or new ideas. The pressure to meet immediate demands stifles creativity, limiting the company's ability to evolve and stay ahead of the competition.

Leaders must actively foster a culture where innovation isn't an afterthought—it's a priority. If your team is only focused on solving today's problems, no one is looking ahead to the future. As a leader, it's your job to drive that train. You must create space for long-term thinking, encourage brainstorming, and ensure that workloads are manageable enough for your team to innovate rather than just survive.

History is filled with examples of companies that innovated not because their leaders had all the answers but because they actively sought insights from others. Steve Jobs sought inspiration from artists and calligraphers, leading to Apple's groundbreaking design principles. Howard Schultz, the CEO of Starbucks, studied Italian coffee culture to transform Starbucks into a global brand. These leaders scaled their companies not by working in isolation but by drawing on the expertise and knowledge of others.

OVERCOMING THE FEAR OF ASKING FOR HELP

For many leaders, the biggest barrier to seeking help is fear—fear of appearing weak, fear of relinquishing control, or fear of being judged. However, the most successful leaders understand that vulnerability is a strength. Admitting that you don't have all the answers fosters authenticity and credibility. Employees respect leaders who are honest about their limitations but proactive in finding solutions.

To overcome this fear, leaders must shift their mindset. Instead of viewing help-seeking as a deficiency, they should see it as a strategic advantage. Organizations thrive when leaders are willing to learn, adapt, and embrace the collective wisdom of their teams and networks. Scaling a business is not about proving you can do everything alone—it's about assembling the right people to achieve something greater together.

SCALING WITH STRENGTH FOR THE FUTURE

Scaling an organization is a complex, dynamic process that no leader can navigate alone. The strongest leaders are those who recognize the value of collaboration, mentorship, and delegation. They understand that sustainable success is built on trust, expertise, and a willingness to seek help when needed. By surrounding themselves with capable teams, leveraging the wisdom of mentors and advisors, and fostering a culture of shared leadership, business leaders can scale effectively while maintaining balance and perspective. The ability to say, "I need help" is not a weakness—it is one of the most powerful leadership skills there is.

Finally, one final thought on this topic—succession planning cannot start soon enough. With everything else demanding your attention, it's easy to push it to the back burner, but it should always be top of mind. What happens if Bob, your key executive, gets hit by a truck? What if Bob finds a better opportunity? What if Bob decides to trade in his suit for a jumpsuit and become an airshow pilot? The reality is, people leave, plans change, and businesses must be prepared.

Succession planning is not just a contingency measure; it's a critical component of long-term stability. A strong leader doesn't just focus on the present—they anticipate the future and ensure the right people are in place to carry the organization forward. CEOs should work with HR professionals to develop a comprehensive plan that identifies and grooms future leaders. And this doesn't just apply to the CEO role—it's essential for every key position in the company. Without a succession strategy, you're not just risking disruption; you're risking the future of the business.

In the next chapter, we'll explore another crucial component of successful scaling: **Creeping Excellence**—the art of continuous improvement and small, intentional advancements that lead to transformational growth.

6

CREEPING EXCELLENCE – THE POWER OF CONTINUOUS IMPROVEMENT IN SCALING SUCCESS

Scaling a business is often portrayed as an explosive, high-speed endeavor—capturing market share, hiring rapidly, and making bold moves. However, the most successful and enduring companies don't scale in a single leap. Instead, they evolve steadily, improving their systems, processes, and products over time with continuous improvement. "Creeping excellence" has negative connotations in the military, law enforcement, and elite special operation units. This usually is not a good thing. It usually means, "It was hard for me when I did it. So it should be even harder for you nowadays."

Creeping excellence should be watched for and stopped immediately or you may limit or preclude good people who would be qualified for the job. The power of small, incremental improvements that compound over time can make a business stronger and more agile and add stability for all the employees. Continuous improvement is the steady, deliberate pursuit of excellence that ensures businesses grow with quality, resilience, and consistency rather than crumbling under the weight of unchecked expansion. It's also intertwined with your team and the individuals working within your organization.

One common pattern I've observed in both the government and the private sector is the phenomenon of creeping excellence in the selection processes of employees or team members. Put simply, it's the slow, often unnoticed rise in standards and expectations for selecting job candidates—whether for jobs, academic programs, or other opportunities. Over time, what was once considered exceptional becomes the new baseline, making it increasingly difficult for individuals to meet ever-evolving criteria. This is a critical problem if left unchecked in a company.

Many leaders overlook creeping excellence and focus on continuous improvement. This must be avoided. Continuous improvement also has its naysayer because it lacks the immediate gratification of rapid growth. In a results-driven world where success is often measured by quarterly earnings, market dominance, or rapid scaling, incremental improvements can seem too slow or insignificant. Leaders may feel pressured—by investors, boards, or even their own ambitions—to chase big wins rather than focusing on the foundational refinements that create long-term stability. The allure of making bold moves, expanding aggressively, or launching new products at breakneck speed can overshadow the importance of fine-tuning existing processes. As a result, organizations prioritizing short-term gains over steady progress often deal with operational inefficiencies, employee burnout, and an inability to sustain growth.

Another reason leaders can ignore continuous improvement in any company is that it requires patience, discipline, and a willingness to invest in long-term improvements rather than immediate returns. Many executives are drawn to grand visions and sweeping transformations, but creeping excellence demands a more methodical approach that prioritizes optimization over disruption. It requires an ongoing commitment to monitoring performance, refining strategies, and making seemingly small changes that, over time, lead to significant advancements. For some leaders, this can feel too incremental, too slow, or even too tedious. Yet, history has shown that companies that adopt a mindset of continuous improvement are the ones that achieve lasting success, outpacing competitors that rely on flashy, short-lived growth spurts.

WHY EXCELLENCE TAKES TIME

Many leaders fall into the trap of thinking that scaling is about massive shifts—big hires, aggressive market expansion, or rapid technological overhauls. While bold moves have their place, sustainable scaling happens when organizations commit to continuous, incremental improvements. Companies that chase fast growth without solidifying their foundation often struggle with inefficiencies, customer dissatisfaction, and operational breakdowns.

Focused continuous improvement is the antidote to reckless scaling. It is about refining processes, hiring higher-quality candidates, improving employee skills, enhancing product quality, and fine-tuning customer experiences—step by step. The organizations that embrace this philosophy don't just grow; they get better as they grow. Each improvement builds upon the last, creating an upward spiral of efficiency and innovation.

Furthermore, continuous improvement fosters resilience. Businesses that scale too quickly without refining their core processes often struggle to adapt when faced with unforeseen challenges. However, those who grow through steady, incremental improvements develop a strong foundation that enables them to pivot when necessary. This adaptability ensures that an organization can weather market fluctuations, shifting consumer preferences, and competitive pressures while maintaining its trajectory toward sustainable success.

THE UPS AND DOWNS OF HIRING FOR EXCELLENCE

I've seen creeping excellence needlessly eliminate strong candidates in both the government and private sectors, shutting out talented individuals who could have made a meaningful impact. While raising standards can elevate an organization's overall quality, it can also create unintended barriers that limit opportunity and diversity. Whether creeping excellence is beneficial or harmful depends entirely on how it is managed and perceived by stakeholders.

On the positive side, higher standards can lead to the selection of top-tier candidates, ensuring that only the most qualified individuals are chosen. In industries where precision and expertise are critical—such as medicine, engineering, and research—this can enhance overall performance and innovation. When managed properly, raising the bar ensures that organizations are staffed with professionals who meet the highest expectations.

However, creeping excellence can also introduce significant challenges. As selection criteria become increasingly demanding, many otherwise capable candidates may struggle to meet the new expectations. This can make the process more competitive and stressful, discouraging qualified individuals from applying altogether. In some cases, it can even create a perception of exclusivity, where only those with specific privileges—such as access to elite education or extensive professional networks—can succeed.

Another major risk is the narrowing of diversity within an organization. As standards become more rigid, the talent pool may shrink to include only those from certain backgrounds or experiences. This lack of diversity can ultimately harm the organization by limiting fresh perspectives, creative problem-solving, and adaptability. When creeping excellence becomes unchecked, it can inadvertently stifle innovation rather than promote it.

THE POWER OF SMALL IMPROVEMENTS

History has shown that businesses prioritizing gradual, persistent improvement outperform those chasing rapid, unsustainable expansion. Toyota, for example, revolutionized the auto industry through the Toyota Production System, a framework built on kaizen, the Japanese philosophy of continuous improvement. Instead of overhauling entire systems overnight, Toyota focused on eliminating waste, improving efficiency, and refining processes incrementally. Over time, these small refinements compounded, making Toyota one of the most successful and respected manufacturers in the world.

Similarly, Amazon didn't become a retail giant overnight. Founder Jeff Bezos famously emphasized the importance of long-term thinking and incremental progress. From refining their logistics networks to improving customer service processes, Amazon scaled by relentlessly enhancing operations one step at a time. Even as they expanded into new industries, they maintained their focus on refining core elements—ensuring that each improvement served as a building block for the next phase of growth.

Likewise, hiring "up" should also be incremental, avoiding the pitfalls of creeping excellence. When organizations raise hiring standards too quickly or dramatically, they risk creating unrealistic expectations that narrow the talent pool to an unsustainable degree. Instead of continuously seeking candidates who check every possible box, companies should focus on steady, intentional improvements in their hiring processes.

Incremental hiring means identifying the most critical skills and qualities needed for a role and gradually refining expectations over time, rather than abruptly setting unattainable criteria. This approach ensures that organizations continue attracting top talent without unnecessarily eliminating capable candidates who, with the right support and development, could grow into the role.

When hiring standards creep too high, organizations may find themselves struggling to fill key positions, leading to stagnation or operational strain. The goal should be progress, not perfection—hiring individuals who meet core needs today while demonstrating the potential to develop into future leaders. Incremental hiring allows companies to scale smartly, ensuring that excellence is achieved through growth, not exclusion.

THE COMPOUNDING EFFECT OF
INCREMENTAL PROGRESS

Small improvements may not seem transformative in the moment, but their long-term impact is undeniable. When organizations focus on marginal gains—improving efficiency by 1%, enhancing customer service by a small margin, or optimizing internal communication—these small wins accumulate into significant competitive advantages. This compounding effect ensures that a company doesn't just get bigger as it scales but gets stronger, more agile, and more resilient.

This approach also minimizes risk. Instead of making sweeping changes that may disrupt operations or alienate employees, creeping excellence allows for gradual adjustments, providing time to measure impact and refine strategies along the way. It prevents organizations from outpacing their own capabilities and ensures that growth is supported by a stable foundation.

By embracing a philosophy of continuous improvement, organizations also build a culture of accountability and ownership at every level. When employees see that even small improvements are valued and contribute to long-term success, they become more engaged in finding efficiencies, refining processes, and innovating within their roles. This mindset creates a ripple effect, where teams are continuously looking for ways to enhance performance rather than waiting for major overhauls or top-down directives. Over time, this culture of incremental progress becomes embedded in the organization's DNA, fostering a workplace where adaptability and sustained excellence drive every decision.

How to Implement Continuous Improvement in Leadership isn't just an operational philosophy—it's a leadership mindset. Leaders who prioritize small, meaningful improvements cultivate a culture of continuous learning and refinement. Here's how they do it:

- Encourage a mindset of iteration: Instead of pushing for perfection immediately, leaders should foster an environment where teams feel empowered to make continuous improvements. Whether it's refining a workflow, enhancing product features, or improving internal communication, the goal should be steady progress rather than drastic overhauls.

- Celebrate small wins: Recognizing incremental achievements reinforces the importance of ongoing improvement. Leaders who acknowledge and reward progress—no matter how minor—build momentum and keep their teams motivated.

- Listen and adapt: Organizations that embrace creeping excellence stay agile by consistently listening to employee feedback, customer insights, and industry trends. Leaders should create mechanisms for continuous feedback and be willing to adjust strategies based on real-world input.

- Invest in long-term growth: Sustainable scaling isn't about quick wins; it's about creating systems and processes that stand the test of time. This means investing in employee development, refining operational efficiencies, and prioritizing long-term customer relationships over short-term profits.

CONTINUOUS IMPROVEMENT IN ACTION: REAL-WORLD EXAMPLES

Continuous Improvement is not just a theoretical concept—it is a proven strategy that some of the world's most successful companies have embraced to achieve sustainable growth. Instead of making drastic changes or taking unnecessary risks, these companies focused on gradual, deliberate improvements that strengthened their operations over time. By refining processes, enhancing customer experience, and prioritizing long-term value over short-term gains, they were able to scale while maintaining quality and consistency. Two notable examples of this approach in action are Starbucks and Nike, both of which grew into global powerhouses through steady, incremental advancements.

Starbucks' rise to a global coffee empire didn't happen overnight. Instead of expanding recklessly, Starbucks prioritized gradual, intentional improvements in its customer experience, product offerings, and store design. CEO Howard Schultz focused on building a culture of quality and consistency, ensuring that every store maintained the same high standards no matter where it opened.

One of Starbucks' most notable examples of creeping excellence was its decision to refine its barista training programs. Instead of simply hiring more staff to meet demand, Schultz invested in comprehensive training programs to enhance the quality of customer service. This commitment to excellence helped Starbucks maintain its reputation as a premium coffee brand, even as it expanded worldwide. Rather than prioritizing speed, the company focused on sustainable scaling—ensuring that every new store upheld its core values and quality standards.

Nike is another company that scaled through continuous improvement rather than immediate disruption. While it is a household name today, its success didn't come from one groundbreaking moment. Instead, Nike consistently refined its product designs, marketing strategies, and supply chain efficiency.

A key example of Continuous Improvement at Nike was its decision to continuously iterate on shoe technology. Rather than overhauling its designs overnight, Nike introduced small but meaningful innovations—such as Flyknit technology, better cushioning, and improved sustainability practices. These incremental changes helped Nike maintain its dominance in the athletic apparel industry while ensuring that each product iteration offered genuine improvements for customers.

WHY CONTINUOUS IMPROVEMENT WINS OVER TIME

Organizations that scale with continuous improvements develop a competitive edge that is difficult to replicate. While competitors may experience rapid bursts of growth, they often struggle with sustainability. Companies that prioritize incremental improvement, however, establish long-term stability, customer loyalty, and operational efficiency.

This methodical, focused approach also fosters adaptability. The business landscape is constantly changing, and companies that scale too quickly often find themselves unable to adjust when challenges arise. Those that grow through small, consistent improvements, however, develop the agility to pivot, refine, and strengthen their position in the market.

Organizations also cultivate a culture of continuous learning and innovation by embracing continuous improvements. Employees become accustomed to refining processes, seeking out efficiencies, and improving their skills over time, which leads to a more engaged and proactive workforce. Instead of reacting to crises or scrambling to fix systemic inefficiencies after rapid expansion, companies that prioritize steady progress are always improving, always iterating, and always positioning themselves for long-term success. This mindset strengthens internal operations and ensures that the organization remains competitive and relevant in an ever-evolving market.

BALANCING EXCELLENT WITH INCLUSIVITY

Balancing excellence with inclusivity is one of the greatest challenges in managing continuous improvements alongside creeping excellence. While high standards drive performance and innovation, organizations must also ensure that their selection processes remain accessible and inclusive. When executed thoughtfully, this balance creates a diverse, dynamic environment where talent is recognized not just by rigid qualifications but by potential, adaptability, and long-term value.

Unchecked creeping excellence can also have unintended consequences on morale. When expectations rise too sharply or become unrealistic, candidates and employees may feel discouraged, believing that success is unattainable. This can lead to frustration, disengagement, and even talent attrition. Organizations must be mindful of this and take proactive steps to provide support, mentorship, and growth opportunities that motivate individuals rather than exclude them.

Collaboration and communication among key stakeholders—including leadership teams, hiring managers, and external advisors—are essential for maintaining fairness in the selection process. Transparency builds trust, and when employees and candidates understand the reasoning behind evolving standards, they are more likely to embrace change rather than resist it.

Finally, ethical considerations must remain at the forefront of any decision to raise standards. Selection criteria should be fair, transparent, and free from bias to prevent unintentional discrimination or systemic barriers. Creeping excellence should be a tool for progress, not exclusion—one that strengthens organizations by ensuring both high performance and equitable opportunity.

SCALING SMART WITH CREEPING EXCELLENCE

Sustainable scaling isn't about speed—it's about precision. The best organizations understand that growth is not a race to the top but a journey of continuous improvement. By embracing methodical growth, businesses can scale in a way that strengthens their foundation, improves quality, and builds long-term resilience.

For leaders, the challenge is clear: Resist the temptation to chase rapid expansion at the expense of quality.

Instead, commit to the small, strategic improvements that will set the stage for sustainable success. Scaling smart means scaling with intention, methodical, and constant, and creeping excellence is something to watch out for and be very wary of if not kept in check.

In the next chapter, we'll explore another critical factor in sustainable growth: Power vs. Control—understanding when to lead with influence versus when to enforce authority and how the right balance can make or break a scaling organization.

7

POWER VS. CONTROL – HOW LEADERSHIP DRIVES SCALING SUCCESS

Scaling a business is not just about systems, strategy, or financial investment—it's about leadership. How a leader wields power can either accelerate or hinder an organization's growth. Too often, leaders equate power with control, believing that keeping a firm grip on every decision will ensure success. However, true leadership is not about controlling every aspect of the business but empowering people to take ownership, make decisions, and drive progress. The most successful organizations scale because their leaders understand the delicate balance between providing strategic oversight and allowing autonomy.

One of leadership's most misunderstood and misused concepts is the distinction between power and control. Many leaders mistakenly believe that maintaining tight control over every decision, process, and outcome is the key to success. They equate authority with micromanagement, assuming that their involvement in every detail will ensure efficiency and prevent mistakes. However, this mindset not only limits the organization's potential but also stifles innovation, erodes trust, and slows progress. The irony is that true power in leadership comes not from control but influence—the ability to inspire, guide, and empower others to take ownership and drive results. Leaders who fail to recognize this fundamental truth often find themselves overwhelmed, struggling to scale, and dealing with disengaged teams that lack the confidence to make meaningful contributions. Understanding this distinction is critical for any leader who wants to build a resilient, scalable organization that thrives in the long run.

THE DIFFERENCE BETWEEN POWER AND CONTROL

At its core, power is the ability to influence and inspire. Conversely, control is about restriction—limiting decision-making to a select few and creating bottlenecks that slow innovation and progress. Leaders who rely on control attempt to manage every detail, believing their involvement is necessary for success. While this approach may work in a small business or startup phase, it becomes a liability as the company grows.

In contrast, leaders who embrace power as a tool for empowerment create organizations that thrive. They build teams that take initiative, make informed decisions, and contribute to the company's vision. Instead of hoarding authority, they distribute it strategically, ensuring that people at all levels have the confidence and autonomy to act. This kind of leadership fosters an environment of trust and collaboration, where employees feel valued and capable of making impactful contributions to the company's growth.

Here are five key examples that illustrate the difference between power and control in leadership:

- **Decision-Making:** A leader who wields power enables their team to make decisions within a clear framework, trusting them to execute. A leader who relies on control insists on approving every decision, creating bottlenecks and slowing progress.

- **Employee Development:** A leader with power invests in mentoring and coaching, helping employees grow into stronger decision-makers. A leader who exerts control micromanages every task, preventing employees from developing their own problem-solving skills.

- **Innovation:** Leaders who embrace power foster a culture where employees feel safe taking calculated risks and experimenting with new ideas. Leaders who rely on control shut down new approaches, fearing change and preferring to stick with rigid structures.

- **Organizational Agility:** A leader with power builds an adaptable organization by trusting teams to adjust strategies as needed. A leader obsessed with control resists change, making it difficult for the organization to pivot in response to challenges.

- **Culture and Morale:** Power-driven leaders create an environment of trust, where employees feel valued and motivated. Control-driven leaders breed resentment, as employees feel stifled, undervalued, and disengaged from the company's vision.

POWER VS. CONTROL IN LEADERSHIP: A REAL-WORLD SCENARIO

Navigating the balance between power and control in leadership isn't always straightforward. To illustrate the difference, let's walk through a scenario involving ABC Corporation as it prepares to launch a new product. The company's two senior leaders— Bob, the CEO, and Jane, the Chief Operating Officer (COO)—approach the project with distinct leadership styles, showcasing how power and control play different but equally important roles.

Bob, the CEO, embodies *power* by inspiring and motivating his team. He understands that a successful product launch requires more than just logistical execution—it requires belief, enthusiasm, and alignment around a shared vision. Bob holds a series of meetings to articulate the product's potential impact, connecting it to the company's long-term goals. He leverages his industry expertise to provide insight while also drawing on his strong relationships with employees to build excitement. Rather than micromanaging, Bob empowers his team, encouraging them to take ownership of their responsibilities and contribute their ideas freely. His influence fosters a culture of creativity, engagement, and high morale, ensuring his employees feel invested in the product's success.

Jane, the COO, takes a *control-driven* approach, focusing on execution and precision. She knows that while vision and motivation are critical, a lack of structure can derail even the best ideas. Jane creates a detailed project plan, setting clear milestones and deadlines to keep the launch on track. She ensures that processes are followed, policies are upheld, and quality control measures are in place. Jane conducts regular check-ins, providing structured feedback and making necessary adjustments along the way. Her control-oriented leadership style keeps the team accountable and ensures no detail is overlooked.

Both Bob and Jane bring essential leadership qualities to the table. Bob's use of power creates an environment where employees feel inspired and engaged, while Jane's control provides the discipline and structure needed to execute efficiently. The balance between their approaches is what makes the product launch successful—Bob's influence ensures the team remains motivated, while Jane's oversight guarantees that the execution stays on course.

This scenario highlights a crucial leadership lesson: power and control are not opposing forces, but complementary tools. Power builds momentum and drives innovation when used effectively, while control ensures that execution is disciplined and reliable. The key is knowing when to inspire and when to enforce, when to trust, and when to tighten the reins. The best leaders don't just choose one approach—they master the balance between both.

WHY CONTROL STIFLES GROWTH

Many leaders struggle to relinquish control because they fear mistakes, inconsistency, or a decline in quality. While these concerns are understandable, excessive control can create far more damage than it prevents. When leaders micromanage, they inadvertently slow decision-making, create inefficiencies, and foster a culture of dependency rather than initiative.

One of the biggest consequences of a control-driven leadership style is the lack of agility. In a fast-scaling organization, speed and adaptability are crucial. If every decision must be approved by the leader, the company's ability to respond to challenges or seize opportunities is severely compromised. Employees become hesitant to take risks, fearing that any deviation from the leader's expectations will result in criticism. Over time, this creates a culture of compliance rather than innovation, where people follow orders rather than think creatively about improving the business.

Additionally, a control-heavy leadership style limits scalability. No leader, no matter how talented, can single-handedly manage every aspect of a growing organization. The leader's bandwidth becomes stretched as the company expands, leading to burnout and missed opportunities. Delegation is not just about lightening the load—it's about ensuring the company has the structural capacity to sustain growth without dependence on a single individual.

Another significant drawback of excessive control is employee disengagement. When employees feel that their opinions and expertise are not valued, they disengage from their work. Instead of proactively solving problems or identifying opportunities, they wait for direction, ultimately slowing the organization's overall progress. This lack of engagement can lead to higher turnover rates as top talent seeks opportunities where they feel empowered and trusted.

THE POWER OF EMPOWERMENT

In contrast to control, effective leadership is about empowerment. Empowered employees take initiative, confidently make decisions, and feel a sense of ownership over their work. This level of engagement and accountability is what fuels scalable growth. When people believe they have a voice and the ability to make an impact, they are more motivated, innovative, and invested in the company's success.

Empowering employees doesn't mean stepping away entirely—it means providing the tools, guidance, and strategic vision they need to succeed. Leaders who master this approach set clear expectations, define key performance indicators, and provide the necessary resources while allowing teams the freedom to execute their responsibilities in the best way they see fit.

One of the most powerful ways to empower employees is through decision-making autonomy. Instead of requiring approval for every action, leaders should establish clear frameworks that allow employees to make informed choices. This not only speeds up execution but also builds confidence and problem-solving skills within the team. When employees feel trusted, they take greater accountability for their work, leading to improved efficiency and higher-quality outcomes.

LEADERS SHOULD NOT FEAR GIVING UP CONTROL

A leader's fear of relinquishing control is one of the greatest barriers to scaling a business. Many leaders worry that if they step back, things will fall apart—employees will make mistakes, standards will decline, or critical decisions will be mishandled. This fear often stems from the early days of building a company when leaders had to be deeply involved in every aspect of the business. However, as an organization grows, holding onto this level of control becomes counterproductive and, ultimately, unsustainable.

Letting go of control does not mean letting go of responsibility. Strong leaders recognize that their role evolves over time. Instead of being involved in every decision, they focus on setting a vision, empowering capable team members, and providing strategic guidance. When leaders learn to trust their teams and delegate effectively, they free up valuable time and energy to focus on higher-level priorities that drive long-term growth.

Fear of delegation often comes from a lack of trust, but trust is built through clarity, communication, and accountability. Leaders who establish clear expectations, provide the necessary tools and resources, and create a feedback-rich environment set their teams up for success. Employees who feel trusted and supported are likelier to take ownership of their work, make thoughtful decisions, and contribute to the company's success in meaningful ways.

Great leadership is not about maintaining control over every detail—it's about creating a culture where people are empowered to take initiative and lead within their own areas of expertise. Leaders who embrace this mindset find that letting go of unnecessary control is not a loss but a gain. It fosters a stronger, more engaged workforce, accelerates decision-making, and allows the organization to scale confidently and efficiently.

REAL-WORLD EXAMPLES: THE POWER VS. CONTROL DILEMMA

The contrast between power and control is best understood through real-world examples of leaders who either embraced empowerment or fell into the trap of micromanagement. Some of the most successful organizations have scaled because their leaders recognized that true leadership is about influence, not rigid oversight. By trusting their teams, delegating authority, and fostering a culture of autonomy, these leaders positioned their companies for long-term success. On the other hand, leaders who clung to excessive control often found themselves hindering growth, creating bottlenecks, and limiting their organization's ability to adapt. The following examples highlight the critical impact that a leader's approach to power and control can have on the trajectory of a business.

Steve Jobs was a visionary leader, but he was also known for his controlling approach. His relentless pursuit of perfection and hands-on management style played a crucial role in Apple's early success. However, as Apple grew, this control-based leadership created tension within the organization. While Jobs' obsession with detail resulted in groundbreaking products, his need to oversee every aspect of the business often slowed decision-making and stifled collaboration.

When Tim Cook took over as CEO, he embraced a different leadership approach based on empowerment rather than control. Cook delegated more authority to his leadership team, trusting them to drive product development and strategic initiatives. This shift maintained Apple's high standards and enabled the company to scale in new directions. Under Cook's leadership, Apple expanded into new markets, launched innovative services, and sustained its position as a global leader in technology. The transition from a control-based model to an empowerment-driven approach was instrumental in Apple's continued growth.

Howard Schultz, the former CEO of Starbucks, also understood that scaling a business wasn't about maintaining control over every detail—it was about empowering people at every level of the organization. From baristas to regional managers, Schultz fostered a culture of ownership, ensuring employees felt invested in the company's success.

One of the key ways Starbucks achieved this was through employee development programs and leadership training. Rather than dictating how every store should operate, Schultz trusted his teams to make decisions aligned with Starbucks' mission and values. This empowerment enhanced customer experience and enabled rapid, sustainable expansion. By shifting from a control-based approach to a culture of empowerment, Starbucks could scale while maintaining its reputation for quality and service.

SCALING THROUGH LEADERSHIP, NOT CONTROL

The difference between power and control is the difference between stagnation and sustainable growth. Leaders who seek to control every aspect of their business will ultimately slow down their success, creating bottlenecks, limiting innovation, and overburdening themselves. In contrast, leaders who leverage their power to empower others build organizations that scale efficiently and sustainably.

Scaling isn't about micromanagement—it's about leadership. The most effective leaders understand that their role is not to dictate every move but to create an environment where teams can excel. By shifting from a control-driven mindset to one of empowerment, leaders set the stage for long-term success, ensuring that their businesses continue to grow without being constrained by the limitations of a single individual.

In the next chapter, we'll explore another critical factor in sustainable growth: **The Never-Quit Attitude**—how relentless perseverance and resilience define successful leaders and businesses that scale.

8

NEVER QUIT ATTITUDE – THE RESILIENCE REQUIRED TO SCALE

Scaling a business is never a straight path. It is filled with unexpected challenges, setbacks, and moments where even the most determined leaders question whether to keep going. The difference between those who scale successfully and those who don't often comes down to one key trait: resilience. The ability to persist in the face of adversity, adapt when necessary, and keep moving forward despite obstacles defines great leaders. Those who embrace a "Never Quit" attitude understand that setbacks are not the end of the road but rather opportunities to learn, refine their approach, and emerge stronger.

RESILIENCE: THE ULTIMATE LEADERSHIP ADVANTAGE

In the world of business, resilience is often an overlooked trait. Many leadership books focus on strategy, execution, and innovation, but few emphasize the importance of mental toughness. The reality is that no matter how brilliant a business model is, how well-funded a company might be, or how skilled its leadership team is, challenges will arise. Market conditions shift, unexpected competitors emerge, internal failures occur, and economic downturns threaten progress. Leaders who lack resilience are often the first to fold under pressure, while those who embrace perseverance and adaptability find ways to push forward.

Resilience is not just about enduring hardship; it's about the mindset leaders bring to adversity. Instead of viewing challenges as insurmountable, resilient leaders see them as problems to solve. They refuse to let short-term failures define their long-term success and continuously seek ways to pivot, innovate, and find new paths to progress. This ability to stay composed, make thoughtful decisions under pressure, and maintain a forward-thinking approach is what enables organizations to survive and thrive in times of uncertainty.

WHY MOST LEADERS STRUGGLE WITH RESILIENCE

Despite its importance, resilience is not an inherent trait—it must be developed. Many leaders struggle with resilience because they are conditioned to associate failure with weakness. From an early stage in their careers, they are rewarded for success and penalized for mistakes. This creates a fear-based mentality where leaders avoid risk, play it safe, and hesitate to make bold decisions that could lead to short-term setbacks but long-term rewards.

Additionally, many leaders lack the coping mechanisms needed to handle stress, failure, and uncertainty. Without a strong support system, whether it be mentors, peer networks, or mental resilience practices, leaders can quickly become overwhelmed when faced with setbacks. This is why some of the most successful leaders prioritize mental and emotional well-being, ensuring they have the endurance necessary to navigate the inevitable ups and downs of scaling a business.

Another challenge is that many leaders struggle with self-awareness, failing to recognize when their own fears and insecurities are holding them back. Resilience requires an honest assessment of one's limitations, an ability to seek help when needed, and a willingness to adjust perspectives when faced with obstacles. Leaders who are unwilling to acknowledge their vulnerabilities often find themselves stuck, repeating the same mistakes rather than learning from them. By developing greater self-awareness, leaders can take proactive steps to strengthen their resilience and cultivate a mindset that embraces growth and adaptability.

THE THREE PILLARS OF A NEVER QUIT ATTITUDE

To cultivate a Never Quit attitude, leaders must develop resilience across three key areas:

Mindset, Adaptability, and Endurance.

MINDSET: EMBRACING CHALLENGES AS OPPORTUNITIES

One of the hallmarks of resilient leaders is their ability to reframe challenges. Instead of seeing difficulties as roadblocks, they view them as stepping stones to growth. This shift in mindset is critical because it changes how leaders approach obstacles—rather than being discouraged by adversity, they become energized by it.

Reframing challenges means shifting how we perceive obstacles—not as threats or failures but as opportunities for growth and learning. It requires a conscious effort to move beyond frustration and see difficulties as valuable experiences that provide insight and build resilience. Instead of viewing setbacks as roadblocks, resilient leaders ask, "What can we learn from this?" or "How can this challenge make us stronger?" This mindset shift allows them to stay proactive rather than reactive, transforming adversity into a tool for continuous improvement. By reframing challenges, leaders cultivate a culture where setbacks are not feared but embraced as essential stepping stones toward long-term success.

Resilient leaders not only reframe challenges but also keep an eye on new opportunities that arise from adversity. Every obstacle presents a chance to pivot, innovate, or uncover untapped potential. Leaders who maintain a forward-thinking approach don't just focus on solving immediate problems—they look beyond them to identify strategic advantages. Whether it's entering a new market, refining a product, or restructuring operations for greater efficiency, challenges often reveal possibilities that wouldn't have been considered otherwise. By staying open to new opportunities, leaders ensure that their organizations remain dynamic, adaptable, and well-positioned for sustainable growth.

ADAPTABILITY: THE WILLINGNESS TO PIVOT

Resilient leaders are not rigid in their thinking. They recognize when a strategy isn't working and have the courage to pivot rather than persist in the wrong direction. This ability to remain flexible while staying committed to a long-term vision is what separates successful organizations from those that stagnate.

One of the most famous examples of adaptability in leadership is Netflix. Originally a DVD rental service, the company faced an existential crisis when streaming technology began to gain traction. Rather than clinging to its original business model, Netflix completely transformed its approach, becoming the world's leading streaming service. This level of adaptability required leadership to accept that their initial model was no longer viable and have the courage to move in an entirely new direction. Leaders who embrace adaptability understand that staying the course is important—but so is knowing when to change it.

Leaders must cultivate a mindset of continuous learning and curiosity to keep yourself in a position to adapt and avoid getting stuck. This means actively seeking out new information, staying attuned to market trends, and surrounding yourself with diverse perspectives that challenge your assumptions. Regularly engaging with mentors, industry experts, and frontline employees ensures that you're not operating in an echo chamber but instead receiving valuable insights that help you make informed decisions. Leaders should also build flexibility into their strategies—rather than committing rigidly to a single path; they should develop multiple contingency plans and be willing to pivot when necessary. Maintaining a habit of reflection, such as periodically evaluating whether current strategies are still effective, prevents complacency and keeps the organization agile. Most importantly, leaders must embrace a mindset where change is not feared but expected, allowing them to remain proactive rather than reactive in an ever-evolving business landscape.

ENDURANCE: PUSHING FORWARD WHEN IT'S HARDEST

Scaling an organization requires long-term perseverance. There will be moments of doubt, financial struggles, and intense competition. What determines success is not just the ability to endure but the willingness to keep pushing forward even when the path is uncertain.

Doubt is inevitable in leadership, especially when faced with uncertainty, setbacks, or the need to pivot. Instead of ignoring or suppressing doubt, great leaders acknowledge it, analyze it, and use it as a tool for better decision-making. Doubt can signal that something needs to be re-evaluated, whether it's a strategy, a market position, or an internal process. The key is to avoid letting doubt turn into paralysis. Instead, leaders should seek out data, feedback, and trusted advisors to gain clarity and perspective. Viewing doubt as a natural part of growth allows leaders to make more informed choices rather than being held back by fear. Ultimately, the presence of doubt isn't a sign of weakness—it's an opportunity to ask better questions, refine strategies, and build the confidence needed to move forward with conviction.

Take the example of Howard Schultz, the former CEO of Starbucks. When he first sought funding to expand Starbucks, he was rejected by more than 200 investors. Had Schultz given up after the first hundred rejections, Starbucks as we know it today would not exist. His ability to endure, to push past repeated failures and setbacks, ultimately led to one of the most successful global brands in history. The lesson here is simple: those who persist longer than others are often the ones who win.

BUILDING A CULTURE OF RESILIENCE

Leaders who embody resilience also build organizations that reflect this quality. Companies that foster a Never Quit attitude at all levels tend to outperform those that fold under pressure. Resilient organizations thrive in uncertainty, while fragile ones crumble under pressure.

The key difference lies in mindset, adaptability, and culture. Resilient organizations embrace change, viewing challenges as opportunities for growth rather than existential threats. They foster a culture where employees are encouraged to take calculated risks, learn from failure, and continuously improve. These companies invest in strong leadership, prioritize innovation, and create systems that allow for flexibility in decision-making. On the other hand, organizations that lack resilience often resist change, operate reactively instead of proactively, and cling to outdated processes even when they no longer serve the business. Their leadership tends to micromanage, fearing delegation, which leads to slow decision-making and low employee morale. While resilient companies emerge stronger from adversity, fragile ones stagnate, lose market relevance, or, in extreme cases, fail entirely. The ability to navigate uncertainty with confidence and agility is what separates businesses that endure from those that fade away.

Here are some ways leaders can create a culture of resilience within their teams:

- **Encourage Risk-Taking and Learning from Failure:** When employees fear failure, they hesitate to innovate. Leaders who normalize failure as a learning experience encourage creativity and calculated risk-taking.

- **Promote Open Communication:** Organizations with resilient cultures create safe spaces for employees to voice concerns, share challenges, and collaborate on solutions.

- **Support Employee Well-Being:** Scaling is demanding, and burnout is a real threat. Companies prioritizing mental health, work-life balance, and professional development cultivate better-equipped employees to handle challenges.

- **Recognize and Celebrate Perseverance:** Acknowledge employees and teams who push through difficult situations and demonstrate resilience. Rewarding determination reinforces the value of persistence within the organization.

THE NEVER QUIT ATTITUDE DEFINES LONG-TERM SUCCESS

Scaling is not for the faint of heart. It demands leaders who are willing to endure setbacks, embrace uncertainty, and push forward even when success feels far away. The Never Quit attitude is not just about working harder—it's about thinking differently, staying adaptable, and having the mental toughness to navigate the complexities of business growth.

The most successful leaders are not the ones who never face failure but the ones who refuse to let failure define them. They view obstacles as opportunities, setbacks as lessons, and challenges as fuel for greater success. By cultivating resilience, fostering adaptability, and maintaining endurance, leaders can build organizations that not only scale but thrive in the face of adversity.

In the next chapter, we'll explore another crucial element of leadership in scaling organizations: **Virtual Leadership**—how to effectively lead and inspire teams in an increasingly remote and digital business environment.

9

VIRTUAL LEADERSHIP – LEADING AND SCALING IN A REMOTE WORLD

Office walls no longer define the modern workplace. The rise of remote and hybrid work environments has changed how businesses operate, making virtual leadership a crucial skill for scaling organizations. Leaders today are tasked with building strong, high-performing teams that are often spread across multiple time zones, cultures, and communication channels. Success in this new landscape depends on mastering virtual leadership—effectively communicating, fostering company culture, and maintaining alignment across dispersed teams.

Great leadership is not about being physically present; it's about influence, trust, and the ability to inspire action, regardless of location. Leaders who can adapt to the challenges of managing remote teams will be the ones who scale their businesses beyond geographical constraints while maintaining engagement, productivity, and cohesion. Virtual leadership isn't just necessary; it's an opportunity to build more diverse, resilient, and innovative organizations.

THE CORE CHALLENGES OF VIRTUAL LEADERSHIP

Leading in a virtual environment presents challenges that traditional office-based leadership does not. Communication, collaboration, accountability, and culture-building become more complex when employees are not physically together. Leaders must intentionally bridge the gaps created by distance, ensuring that teams remain engaged and aligned with the company's vision.

One of the biggest challenges is the loss of organic interactions. In an office setting, impromptu conversations, quick check-ins, and informal brainstorming sessions happen naturally. In a remote environment, these moments must be recreated deliberately. Leaders must proactively foster connection and ensure employees feel seen, heard, and valued despite the physical distance.

Another challenge is maintaining accountability and productivity without micromanaging. Some leaders struggle with trusting their teams without direct oversight, while others overcompensate by imposing excessive meetings and check-ins, leading to burnout. Effective virtual leadership strikes the right balance between autonomy and accountability, ensuring that employees have the flexibility to work efficiently while staying aligned with organizational goals.

Finally, company culture can suffer in a remote environment if not nurtured properly. In a physical workspace, culture is reinforced through shared experiences, in-person meetings, and the environment itself. When employees work remotely, culture must be built through intentional actions, clear values, and a strong sense of community.

BUILDING STRONG COMMUNICATION IN A VIRTUAL SETTING

Communication is the foundation of effective virtual leadership. Without clear and consistent communication, misunderstandings arise, projects stall, and employees feel disconnected. Leaders must create systems facilitating transparent, open, and structured communication across remote teams.

Over-Communicate with Clarity Unlike in an office, where information spreads organically, remote teams require structured communication to stay informed. Leaders must clearly articulate goals, expectations, and priorities through multiple channels—whether it's email, video meetings, or collaborative tools like Slack and Microsoft Teams. The key is to over-communicate without overwhelming—providing clarity without unnecessary noise.

Choose the Right Communication Tools Different messages require different mediums. A quick update may be best suited for a Slack message, while strategic discussions require face-to-face interaction via video conferencing. Leaders should establish communication norms to ensure that messages are delivered effectively. For example, reserving video calls for important discussions and using asynchronous communication (like recorded video updates or written reports) for less urgent matters prevents meeting fatigue and keeps teams focused.

Foster a Culture of Open Dialogue In a remote setting, it's easy for employees to feel disconnected or hesitant to speak up. Leaders should encourage open discussions, ensuring employees feel comfortable sharing concerns, ideas, and feedback. This can be achieved through regular one-on-one check-ins, anonymous feedback surveys, and open forums where employees can voice their thoughts without fear of judgment.

MAINTAINING COMPANY CULTURE IN A REMOTE ENVIRONMENT

A physical office does not define culture—the people within it define it. In a virtual setting, leaders must work harder to create a culture that keeps employees engaged, motivated, and aligned with company values.

1. **Define and Reinforce Core Values** A strong culture starts with well-defined values. Leaders must ensure that their company's mission, vision, and values are not just written on a website but embedded into daily operations. Regularly reinforcing these values through company-wide meetings, recognition

programs, and leadership messaging helps keep the culture alive.

2. **Create Virtual Rituals and Traditions** Just as in-person teams bond through shared experiences; remote teams need traditions that build connection. Whether it's virtual coffee breaks, team-building exercises, or online celebrations, these moments help employees feel like part of a community rather than isolated workers behind a screen.

3. **Encourage Social Connection** Remote work can feel isolating without intentional social interaction. Leaders should create spaces for informal conversations, whether through dedicated Slack channels for casual chats, virtual happy hours, or team-building activities that bring employees together outside of work tasks.

KEEPING TEAMS ALIGNED AND ACCOUNTABLE

Alignment is critical in a remote environment—without it, teams drift, productivity suffers, and projects lose momentum. Leaders must implement systems that keep everyone focused and accountable.

1. **Set Clear Goals and Expectations** Remote employees need clarity on their roles, responsibilities, and objectives. Leaders should establish key performance indicators (KPIs), clearly

outline expectations, and ensure every employee understands how their work contributes to the bigger picture.

2. **Implement a Results-Oriented Approach** Micromanagement is a common pitfall in virtual leadership. Leaders should measure success based on output and results instead of focusing on how many hours an employee works. A results-oriented approach fosters trust, autonomy, and motivation, allowing employees to focus on meaningful work rather than arbitrary check-ins.

3. **Use Technology to Streamline Accountability** Project management tools like Asana, Trello, or Monday.com help remote teams stay organized and aligned. Leaders should leverage these tools to track progress, assign tasks, and provide visibility into team workloads without excessive meetings.

THE FUTURE OF VIRTUAL LEADERSHIP

Virtual leadership is no longer an option—it's a necessity. As organizations continue to embrace remote and hybrid work models, leaders must refine their ability to manage teams from anywhere in the world. The ability to communicate effectively, build a strong culture, and keep teams aligned in a virtual environment will be a defining skill for modern leaders.

The best virtual leaders understand that leadership is not about physical presence but about influence, trust, and clarity. They invest in the right tools, prioritize people, and lead with empathy, ensuring remote teams are as engaged and productive as in-office teams. Scaling in the digital age requires leaders who can navigate the challenges of remote work while fostering innovation, accountability, and collaboration.

LEADING BEYOND BORDERS

Virtual leadership offers unprecedented opportunities to scale businesses beyond geographical limitations, build diverse global teams, and create flexible work environments that attract top talent. The leaders who master this skill will be the ones who build resilient, adaptable, and high-performing organizations in the modern world.

In the next chapter, we'll explore another crucial component of leadership in scaling organizations: **Emotional Intelligence**—how self-awareness, empathy, and interpersonal skills shape great leaders in virtual and in-person environments.

10

EMOTIONAL INTELLIGENCE – THE HIDDEN DRIVER OF SCALING SUCCESS

As organizations grow, leadership becomes less about technical expertise and more about managing people effectively. Understanding, navigating, and influencing emotions—both one's own and those of others—is at the core of great leadership. Emotional Intelligence (EI) is not a soft skill; it's a foundational component of leading and scaling an organization successfully. Leaders who cultivate high EI can foster collaboration, build trust, and create an environment where employees feel valued and motivated to contribute their best work.

In today's fast-paced, digitally connected world, emotional intelligence is more critical than ever. The rise of remote work, diverse global teams, and rapid technological advancements has fundamentally changed how organizations operate. Leaders must navigate complex interpersonal dynamics without the benefit of in-person interactions, making empathy, active listening, and clear communication essential. Additionally, employees expect more than just financial compensation—they seek purpose, inclusion, and a positive workplace culture. Leaders who cultivate high EI are better equipped to foster engagement, retain top talent, and drive innovation in an environment where human connection remains the most valuable currency.

Scaling a business is not just about strategy and execution; it's about people. The more an organization expands, the more complex its interpersonal dynamics become. Leaders who lack emotional intelligence often struggle with employee engagement, conflict resolution, and maintaining a strong culture. On the other hand, leaders with high EI can navigate these challenges confidently, ensuring their teams remain cohesive, resilient, and adaptable in the face of growth.

WHAT IS EMOTIONAL INTELLIGENCE?

Emotional Intelligence consists of four key components: **self-awareness, self-regulation, social awareness, and relationship management.** These pillars shape how leaders perceive and respond to challenges, interact with employees, and make strategic decisions.

THE ROLE OF EMOTIONAL INTELLIGENCE IN LEADERSHIP

High-EI leaders create an atmosphere of trust, accountability, and open communication. They foster environments where employees feel psychologically safe, knowing that their contributions matter and that their leaders genuinely care about their well-being. There are four key aspects of EI.

Self-Awareness: Leaders must understand their own emotions, strengths, and weaknesses. Self-aware leaders recognize how their emotions impact their decision-making and leadership style, allowing them to lead with clarity and authenticity. Self-awareness also enables leaders to recognize their biases, emotional triggers, and blind spots, helping them make better, more objective decisions. Leaders who cultivate self-awareness seek regular feedback, reflect on their experiences, and continuously work on improving their emotional and behavioral responses. Understanding their limitations makes them more open to collaboration, mentorship, and personal growth.

Self-Regulation: Scaling comes with pressures and stress, but leaders who regulate their emotions remain composed and make rational decisions. Self-regulation prevents reactive decision-making and fosters stability within the organization. Leaders with strong self-regulation do not let stress dictate their actions or allow frustration to cloud their judgment. Instead, they practice patience, mindfulness, and emotional discipline to respond thoughtfully to challenges. This ability to stay composed under pressure sets the tone for the entire organization, creating a culture where employees feel secure, supported, and empowered to navigate difficult situations.

Social Awareness: Leaders must be attuned to their employees' emotions, needs, and concerns. Understanding the collective mindset of a team allows leaders to navigate conflict, provide support, and ensure employees feel heard and valued. Socially aware leaders pay attention to verbal and nonverbal cues, ensuring they recognize when team members are disengaged, frustrated, or struggling. They actively listen, ask insightful questions, and foster inclusivity by acknowledging and respecting diverse perspectives. This heightened sensitivity to team dynamics helps leaders address concerns before they escalate, build trust, and create an environment where employees feel genuinely understood.

Relationship Management: Strong relationships are the backbone of an organization. Leaders with high EI build meaningful connections, communicate effectively, and foster team collaboration. They know how to navigate difficult conversations and resolve conflicts without damaging morale. Effective relationship management goes beyond networking—it requires leaders to invest time in building meaningful, authentic connections with their teams. Leaders who excel in this area foster collaboration across departments, create mentorship opportunities, and help resolve conflicts in a way that strengthens relationships rather than creating divisions. They understand that relationships require ongoing effort and are proactive in nurturing them through regular communication, recognition, and support.

BUILDING A CULTURE OF TRUST AND PSYCHOLOGICAL SAFETY

Trust is the currency of leadership, and emotional intelligence is key to earning it. Employees are likelier to be engaged and productive when they trust their leaders to be honest, fair, and compassionate. Leaders who actively listen, acknowledge concerns and show empathy build workplaces where people feel safe to share ideas and voice concerns without fear of retribution.

Google's Project Aristotle, a multi-year study on high-performing teams, found that the most critical factor in team success was psychological safety—the belief that individuals could take risks and be vulnerable in front of their colleagues. This research underscores the importance of EI in leadership. Leaders who cultivate trust unlock innovation, encourage open dialogue, and strengthen team cohesion.

Indeed, when trust is embedded in an organization's culture, employees feel a stronger sense of loyalty and commitment, leading to higher engagement and lower turnover rates. A workplace where psychological safety thrives fosters collaboration and a willingness to challenge ideas, share creative solutions, and take ownership of projects. Leaders who consistently demonstrate emotional intelligence by being transparent, approachable, and receptive to feedback cultivate resilient and motivated teams. When employees trust their leadership, they are more likely to contribute their best work, support each other, and align themselves with the company's long-term vision.

MANAGING CONFLICT WITH EMOTIONAL INTELLIGENCE

In any growing organization, conflict is inevitable. Whether it's disagreements over strategy, competing priorities, or interpersonal clashes, how a leader handles conflict determines whether it strengthens or weakens the team. Leaders with emotional intelligence address conflicts constructively, focusing on resolution rather than blame.

Instead of reacting emotionally, high-EI leaders approach conflict with curiosity and a willingness to understand different perspectives. They de-escalate tensions, ensure all parties feel heard, and facilitate solutions that align with the organization's goals. When leaders model this behavior, they create a culture where conflict is seen as an opportunity for improvement rather than a source of dysfunction.

MOTIVATING AND INSPIRING TEAMS

Scaling a business requires sustained motivation across all levels of an organization. High-EI leaders recognize that different employees are driven by different factors—some by recognition, others by purpose, and some by growth opportunities. Leaders can drive engagement and productivity by understanding and catering to these motivations.

Emotional intelligence allows leaders to connect with their employees personally, making them feel valued and appreciated. Employees who feel seen and understood are more likely to invest in their work and stay committed to the company's mission. This is particularly critical in high-growth environments, where rapid change can lead to stress and uncertainty.

A leader's ability to sustain motivation also depends on their capacity to communicate a compelling vision that resonates with employees on an emotional level. When people understand how their work contributes to a larger purpose, they are more likely to remain engaged and resilient through periods of change. High-EI leaders reinforce this connection by celebrating big and small wins, recognizing individual contributions, and fostering a culture where employees feel their efforts are meaningful. This emotional reinforcement boosts morale and creates an environment where employees are intrinsically motivated to push through challenges and contribute to the organization's long-term success.

DEVELOPING EMOTIONAL INTELLIGENCE AS A LEADER

Can high-EI be learned? While some individuals naturally possess high EI, emotional intelligence can be developed and refined over time. Leaders who prioritize self-improvement and actively work on enhancing their emotional intelligence will be better equipped to lead effectively at scale. In his seminal book *Emotional Intelligence: Why It Can Matter More Than IQ*, Daniel Goleman asserts that emotional intelligence competencies are learned and can be improved at any point in life. He emphasizes that individuals can enhance their emotional intelligence with motivation and a well-structured learning approach.

Throughout my career, I have intentionally worked on developing my emotional intelligence, recognizing that leadership is as much about managing emotions—both my own and others—as it is about strategy and execution. I have made a conscious effort to become more self-aware, reflecting on how my reactions and decisions impact those around me. I've learned to regulate my emotions under pressure, ensuring that stress or frustration doesn't dictate my leadership approach. Actively listening to my team and seeking feedback has been a crucial part of my growth, allowing me to understand different perspectives and foster stronger relationships. I have also worked on my empathy, ensuring that I hear what people are saying and truly understand their concerns and motivations.

By continuously refining these skills, I've seen first-hand how emotional intelligence strengthens trust, improves communication, and ultimately drives better outcomes in leadership and business. I've discovered four vital ways to keep my emotional intelligence strong:

PRACTICING SELF-REFLECTION

Great leaders take time to reflect on their actions, decisions, and emotional responses. Regular self-reflection allows leaders to recognize patterns in their behavior, identify areas for improvement, and make more intentional choices moving forward. Journaling, meditation, and seeking feedback from trusted colleagues are powerful tools for self-awareness. Leaders who prioritize self-reflection also develop a habit of asking themselves important questions like, *Did I handle that situation in the best way possible?* or *How did my emotions influence my response?* This conscious introspection allows them to fine-tune their leadership approach, ensuring they continuously improve their ability to effectively connect with and lead others. Additionally, leaders who engage in self-reflection create a culture where personal growth and development are valued, encouraging employees to adopt the same mindset.

ACTIVE LISTENING AND EMPATHY

Listening is one of the most undervalued yet powerful leadership skills. Leaders with high EI practice active listening—not just hearing words but truly understanding the emotions and concerns behind them. They ask thoughtful questions, show empathy, and validate employees' experiences. A practical way to develop this skill is by engaging in regular one-on-one meetings with team members, creating open forums for feedback, and demonstrating genuine curiosity about employees' challenges and aspirations. Another way to strengthen active listening is by practicing reflective listening—repeating or summarizing what was said to ensure understanding. This technique reassures employees that their voices are heard and helps prevent miscommunication. Additionally, leaders who approach conversations with genuine curiosity and openness build trust and stronger connections with their teams, leading to better collaboration and workplace morale.

REGULATING EMOTIONAL RESPONSES

Scaling a company often involves high-pressure situations where emotions can run high. Leaders who regulate their emotions maintain composure and make rational, strategic decisions rather than react impulsively. Techniques such as mindfulness, deep breathing exercises, and pausing before responding can help leaders develop better emotional control. Those who master emotional regulation recognize their emotional triggers and actively work to manage them. Instead of reacting with frustration or impatience, they step back, assess the situation logically, and respond with intention. By modeling this behavior, leaders set an example for their teams, creating an environment where calm, solution-oriented thinking is the norm. Encouraging emotional regulation among employees also leads to healthier workplace interactions and minimizes unnecessary conflicts.

LEADING BY EXAMPLE

Employees take behavioral cues from their leaders. If a leader remains calm under pressure, treats others respectfully, and handles challenges with a level head, their team will follow suit. Conversely, leaders who display frustration, dismiss concerns or fail to communicate effectively create an environment of uncertainty and disengagement. Leading by example also means demonstrating a growth mindset—showing a willingness to learn, adapt, and acknowledge mistakes. Leaders who are open about their own development journey foster an organizational culture where continuous improvement is embraced. By maintaining a positive and solution-focused attitude, leaders inspire their teams to approach challenges with resilience, ultimately strengthening the entire organization.

Emotional intelligence, like physical fitness, requires consistent effort and intentional practice. Just as you wouldn't expect to stay in peak physical shape without regular exercise, you can't expect to maintain high EI without actively working on self-awareness, empathy, and emotional regulation. It's a muscle that strengthens over time through reflection, listening, and adapting to new challenges. Leaders who commit to improving their EI—just as they would their physical endurance—become more resilient, adaptable, and effective in navigating the complexities of leadership and scaling an organization.

EMOTIONAL INTELLIGENCE AS A COMPETITIVE ADVANTAGE

Organizations led by emotionally intelligent leaders are more adaptable, innovative, and resilient. EI-driven leadership fosters collaboration, minimizes turnover, and creates teams that are not just high-performing but deeply invested in the company's success. As businesses scale, maintaining strong relationships, ensuring alignment across teams, and preserving company culture become increasingly difficult—making emotional intelligence more valuable than ever.

Some of the world's most successful CEOs, including Satya Nadella of Microsoft, have attributed their leadership success to emotional intelligence. Nadella's leadership philosophy centered on empathy, collaboration, and fostering a growth mindset—qualities that were instrumental in transforming Microsoft's culture and redefining its trajectory. When he took over as CEO in 2014, Microsoft was struggling with internal silos, a rigid, competitive culture, and declining innovation. Rather than focusing solely on financial performance and operational efficiency, Nadella prioritized creating an environment where employees felt empowered, valued, and encouraged to contribute ideas.

By embedding emotional intelligence into Microsoft's leadership approach, Nadella fostered a learning, innovation, and teamwork culture. He emphasized active listening, encouraged open communication, and shifted the company's focus toward customer-centric solutions. He also promoted a "learn-it-all" mentality rather than a "know-it-all" attitude, reinforcing that success comes from continuous learning and adaptability. This cultural transformation revitalized employee engagement and fueled Microsoft's resurgence as a global technology leader. Under Nadella's leadership, the company expanded into cloud computing, artificial intelligence, and other high-growth markets, leading to record-breaking revenues and a market capitalization that soared past $2 trillion.

His success proves that emotional intelligence is not a soft skill—it's a leadership imperative. By prioritizing empathy and collaboration, Nadella didn't just turn Microsoft around; he set a new standard for modern leadership, demonstrating that the most effective leaders are those who inspire and empower their teams rather than control them.

THE ROLE OF EQ IN THE FUTURE OF LEADERSHIP

In an era where technological advancements and remote work continue to redefine the workplace, emotional intelligence remains one of the most critical leadership traits. It is not just a "nice-to-have" skill—it is the foundation of effective leadership in a scaling organization.

Leaders who invest in developing their EI will build stronger teams, foster accountability, and create a culture of trust and collaboration. As organizations grow, those who master emotional intelligence will scale their businesses successfully and leave a lasting impact on the people they lead.

In the next chapter, we'll explore another key aspect of leadership in scaling organizations: **Dealing with Change**—how leaders can navigate uncertainty, drive transformation, and keep their teams engaged in the face of rapid growth.

11

DEALING WITH CHANGE –
EMBRACING THE INEVITABLE

S caling is, at its core, a process of constant change. Organizations that grow successfully are those that evolve—adapting to new markets, expanding teams, implementing new systems, and refining strategies. Leaders who resist change or fail to manage it effectively, risk stagnation or collapse. Change is inevitable, but how a leader navigates it determines whether the organization thrives or struggles.

The most successful leaders understand that change isn't something to fear—it's an opportunity. Businesses that remain agile and adaptable in the face of shifting market conditions, industry disruptions, and internal evolution will sustain growth far longer than those that try to preserve the status quo. However, leading through change isn't just about embracing it at the top; it's about ensuring that teams remain aligned, engaged, and confident in the face of uncertainty.

WHY LEADERS STRUGGLE WITH CHANGE

Even the best leaders can struggle with change because it often brings discomfort, uncertainty, and a loss of control. Many leaders build their businesses based on a winning formula, and when circumstances require them to adjust, there's a natural hesitation. Change means stepping into the unknown, and even the most seasoned executives can feel uncertain when faced with the prospect of altering what has worked in the past.

Fear of failure is another major obstacle. Leaders who have spent years crafting a vision, hiring the right people, and executing successful strategies may worry that change could disrupt progress rather than advance it. However, refusing to evolve is often the bigger risk—companies that fail to adapt to changing conditions are the ones most likely to fall behind.

Finally, many leaders underestimate the emotional toll that change can take on their teams. Employees often resist change, particularly when it threatens job security, shifts established routines, or disrupts team dynamics. Leaders who ignore these concerns or fail to provide clarity only fuel uncertainty, leading to disengagement and decreased morale.

THE CRITICAL ROLE OF COMMUNICATION IN CHANGE MANAGEMENT

One of the biggest reasons organizational change efforts fail is poor communication. Employees don't necessarily fear change itself; rather, they fear the uncertainty that comes with it. When leaders fail to communicate effectively, teams are left guessing, speculating, and often resisting what they don't fully understand. To successfully implement change, leaders must be intentional in how they communicate, ensuring transparency and clarity at every stage of the transition. Without this, even the most well-planned initiatives can fail before they begin.

Before rolling out any major change, leaders must articulate why the change is happening and what the expected outcome will be. Employees need to understand not just what is changing but how it aligns with the company's long-term vision and success. Employees who don't see the bigger picture may view the change as arbitrary, unnecessary, or disruptive. A clear and compelling vision provides direction and purpose, helping employees connect with the transformation rather than resist it. Leaders who fail to communicate this vision effectively risk skepticism, disengagement, and, ultimately, failure in execution.

Delays in communication can be just as harmful as a lack of communication. Waiting too long to announce a major shift fuels employee speculation, misinformation, and unnecessary anxiety. Leaders should proactively communicate upcoming changes as early as possible, allowing teams to process, prepare, and adjust. However, one initial announcement is not enough—ongoing communication is critical. Regular updates through company-wide meetings, emails, and town halls help reinforce key messages and provide clarity throughout the transition. Informal check-ins with employees and managers also allow leaders to address concerns in real time, preventing uncertainty from spreading.

Change should never feel like a top-down mandate imposed without input. Employees who feel their voices are valued are far more likely to support and embrace change. Leaders should actively seek feedback and encourage open discussions about upcoming transitions. When employees have a space to ask questions, share concerns, and contribute ideas, they become active participants in the process rather than reluctant bystanders. Organizations that foster two-way communication build a culture of trust, which makes employees more receptive to change rather than resistant to it.

Transparency is at the core of effective change management. Leaders who are open about both the opportunities and the challenges of change foster credibility and confidence within their teams. Employees don't expect leaders to have all the answers immediately but expect honesty. Acknowledging potential difficulties, addressing concerns head-on, and keeping the lines of communication open can significantly reduce resistance and build collective commitment to the transition.

Change is not just about policies, processes, or technology—it's about people. When leaders prioritize communication, provide a clear vision, and foster a culture of trust and collaboration, they turn change from a disruption into an opportunity. Organizations that master this approach don't just survive transitions; they use them as a catalyst for long-term success and sustainable growth.

CREATING A STRUCTURED TRANSITION PLAN

A structured transition plan helps ensure that change is implemented smoothly and with minimal disruption. Change should not feel chaotic or abrupt; instead, it should be a guided process that provides employees with a clear roadmap for adaptation. Over the course of my career in both the public and private sectors, I have developed a three-pronged plan for managing transitions effectively. This approach focuses on identifying key stakeholders, implementing change in phases, and ensuring employees have the training and support they need to succeed.

Major organizational changes should never rely on a single leader to drive them. Identifying key stakeholders—such as department heads, managers, and influential employees—creates a support system that strengthens the transition. These individuals serve as champions of change, reinforcing messaging, addressing concerns, and providing localized leadership within their teams. When employees see respected leaders within their own ranks advocating for and guiding the transition, they are far more likely to engage positively with the process.

Change is always more manageable when implemented in phases rather than as a sudden overhaul. A gradual rollout allows leaders to test new processes, gather feedback, and make necessary adjustments along the way. Employees also benefit from phased implementation, as it gives them time to acclimate, reducing the risk of feeling overwhelmed. This incremental approach minimizes disruptions and allows leaders to identify and correct issues before they escalate.

To successfully navigate change, employees must have the right tools, resources, and knowledge. Whether the transition involves adopting new technology, restructuring teams, or shifting strategic priorities, leaders must ensure they receive proper training and support. Workshops, Q&A sessions, and mentorship programs help employees develop confidence in new processes. Providing ongoing support fosters a culture of adaptability, ensuring that teams can not only handle change but embrace it as a continuous part of growth.

By integrating these three pillars—stakeholder engagement, phased implementation, and structured training—leaders can create a transition process that feels purposeful rather than disruptive. Change will always come with challenges, but when managed with clarity and strategy, it becomes a force for progress rather than a source of uncertainty.

KEEPING TEAMS ALIGNED AMID UNCERTAINTY

When organizations undergo change, alignment is critical. If different departments and teams move in different directions or operate under different assumptions, chaos ensues. Leaders must work proactively to maintain alignment and cohesion during periods of transformation.

1. REINFORCE CORE VALUES

Even as operational elements of a business evolve, core values should remain consistent. Leaders must emphasize that change does not mean abandoning the company's mission but rather evolving to better serve it. This helps employees stay connected to the organization's larger purpose.

2. CELEBRATE SMALL WINS

Acknowledging progress is essential in maintaining momentum. Leaders should recognize milestones along the way, celebrating small wins that demonstrate the benefits of the change. When employees see tangible success, their confidence in the transition grows.

3. LEAD WITH EMPATHY

Change is emotional. Leaders who acknowledge employees' challenges and provide emotional support during transitions foster a culture of resilience. Checking in with teams, validating concerns, and offering encouragement can significantly affect how well an organization adapts.

COMPANIES THAT SUCCESSFULLY NAVIGATED CHANGE

Some of the world's most successful companies are those that embraced change rather than resisted it. Netflix began as a DVD rental-by-mail service but recognized early on that the future of entertainment was digital. Rather than clinging to its existing business model, Netflix proactively shifted its strategy, investing heavily in streaming technology. This was not an easy transition—subscription pricing changes led to customer pushback, and shifting business operations required a significant overhaul. However, by embracing the changing landscape and innovating, Netflix became a dominant entertainment industry force. Had it resisted change, it likely would have suffered the same fate as Blockbuster.

Also, when Satya Nadella became CEO of Microsoft in 2014, the company struggled with declining relevance. Rather than relying solely on traditional software sales, Nadella embraced cloud computing and shifted the company's focus toward innovation, collaboration, and flexibility. Under his leadership, Microsoft pivoted toward cloud-based solutions, growing its Azure platform and transforming workplace software. By adapting to industry shifts and fostering a culture of learning and experimentation, Microsoft regained its status as a technology leader.

CHANGE AS A COMPETITIVE ADVANTAGE

Change is not a disruption to scaling—it is a fundamental part of it. Organizations that view change as an opportunity rather than a threat position themselves for long-term success. Leaders who communicate effectively, implement structured transition plans, and keep their teams aligned create agile, competitive, and resilient organizations.

Great leaders don't just manage change—they drive it. Those who embrace adaptability and continuous evolution will not only scale their businesses but also build companies that endure shifting markets and unforeseen challenges.

In the next chapter, we'll explore another critical component of leadership in scaling organizations: **Motivational Speaking—How leaders can inspire action, align teams, and rally their organizations behind a shared vision.**

12

MOTIVATIONAL SPEAKING – INSPIRING ACTION THROUGH COMMUNICATION

S caling an organization isn't just about strategy, execution, and operations—it's also about inspiration. A fundamental leadership skill is communicating a compelling vision, energizing a team, and aligning stakeholders. Whether addressing employees, investors, or customers, leaders must master the art of storytelling, persuasion, and motivation to drive collective action. Effective motivational speaking isn't just about delivering polished speeches; it's about fostering belief, instilling confidence, and creating momentum that propels an organization forward.

I want to share a story with you before I share what I've learned about inspiring action through communication. I could start by outlining leadership theories, breaking down frameworks for persuasive speaking, or discussing the mechanics of effective communication—but none of that would hit home the way a real story does. Because leadership isn't just about what you *say*—it's about how you *connect*. It's about the emotions you evoke, the trust you build, and the way you make people *feel*.

Stories have power. They engage people in a way that statistics and directives never can. They create a shared experience, a moment where the listener leans in, not just to hear, but to *feel* the weight of what you're saying. And that's the key to inspiring action.

You don't move people with data points; you move them with meaning. You don't just instruct—you make them *believe*.

So, before I get into the lessons I've learned about leadership and communication, let me tell you about one of the most defining moments of my life and the dramatic impact it had on how I view leadership. It was a moment when the only thing that mattered was survival, when no strategy, no carefully prepared words, and no rehearsed speech could save me. It was just me, the darkness, and the will to keep going. Listen to this story, and then you'll understand what it really means to communicate with impact.

Treading water in the Atlantic Ocean at night, alone, exhausted, and unsure of rescue, is an experience that changes you forever. The vast, endless blackness surrounds you, the relentless waves pulling you up and down like a ragdoll. The cold cuts deep, draining your strength with every passing minute. In those moments when survival is no longer guaranteed, you learn exactly what you are made of.

If you really want to understand what it felt like, put on your clothes, step into the shower, turn on the ice-cold water, and let it drench you. Then, take a deep breath, step into a pitch-black closet, and close the door, sealing out all light with a towel. That's close, but still not quite it. Because the part you can't replicate—the part that makes survival a battle—is the weight of uncertainty pressing against you, the knowledge that no one knows exactly where you are, and the grim realization that if you don't fight, you won't make it.

Helo casting—jumping from a moving helicopter into the ocean—is standard practice in specialized tactical and hostage rescue teams. It's usually calculated and precise: 10 knots forward speed, 10 feet above the water, or zero knots and 15 feet. The key detail? Usually. Everything went sideways that night, off the coast of Key West, Florida, in total darkness.

We were five miles out in a Black Hawk, the wind and rain hammering us as we prepared for the jump. The storm had rolled in, turning the sea into a violent, churning force, waves now cresting at 15 feet. We had trained for this scenario countless times, but training doesn't change physics—water at high speed and from the wrong height might as well be concrete.

Three minutes out, the TAO (Tactical Air Officer) yelled, "Three minutes!" signaling with his fingers. I responded, signaling back three fingers. One minute out. Signal one finger. Thirty seconds. Signal make a "C" shape with your hand. Legs dangling in the open doorway, the rotor wash roaring, my swim buddy and I locked eyes, knowing the rule: You go, I go.

Then I heard the command—Go! I jumped.

Mid-air, I caught something unusual—another voice, shouting, No! But it was too late. Free-falling into the abyss, I instinctively assumed the helo cast position—legs crossed, one hand securing my mask, the other gripping my belt. I started counting. One thousand one, one thousand two... usually by three, I would hit the water. But I kept falling. One thousand four... one thousand five... I was still airborne.

And then—impact.

I hit hard, my left side taking the brunt of the force. Pain exploded through my ribs and shoulder. As I surfaced, gasping for air, I quickly assessed my situation. My mask? Cracked. My right fin? Gone. My GPS unit? Missing. The "Mae West" flotation device strapped to me? Leaking. I wasn't floating—I was sinking. And then, the worst realization of all—my swim buddy wasn't there.

I screamed his name, but the ocean swallowed my voice. The Black Hawk was heading north, its lights flickering as it moved away. My pulse pounded. They don't see me. They don't know where I am.

Instinct kicked in. We always carried chem lights—small glow sticks attached to our wetsuits. Green meant everything was okay, white for general visibility, red for I am in trouble. Without hesitation, I cracked the red stick and waved it above my head. At the peak of a wave, I caught a glimpse of the helicopter. They were circling back. Relief surged through me—I won't be out here long.

Except I would.

The helicopter flew right by. They didn't see me. I was invisible between the towering waves and the rain now pelting down. My arms burned as I kept signaling, but each pass missed me. The ocean was swallowing me whole, and now, seconds turned into minutes, my chem light was dimming—fifteen minutes of glow time was all I had.

I wasn't ready to die that night. I had two options—panic or adapt. I let go of my remaining gear, weapons, ammo, and tactical vest, reducing weight so I could stay afloat longer. My breathing slowed. I focused on every rise and fall of the waves, conserving what little energy I had left. My mind flickered to my training, survival tactics, and anything that would keep me going.

I thought about swimming for Key West—five miles. Doable in calm waters, but with the current? I'd be halfway to Cuba before I knew it. No. Stay put. I'd probably swim in circles with my right fin gone. Stay visible. Survive.

Little did I know, my swim buddy had never jumped. Someone had realized the height was too high because I went in one of the troughs of a wave instead of the top and grabbed him before he could follow. A fight had broken out in the helicopter—You go, I go! Johnny took his role seriously, just as we all did. It was not just a rule; it was a creed, and Johnny was ready to go in after me. They stopped him. But I had no idea. Maybe the current took him or maybe he is hurt. I was alone.

The third pass of the helicopter came. My arms felt like lead, my legs barely kicking against the pull of the waves. I could hear the rotors see the searchlights sweeping, but they weren't seeing me. And then, the noise faded. They were leaving. The red glow of my chem light flickered one last time, then died.

At that moment, in the blackest of nights, with no light, flotation, or sign of rescue, I was left with nothing but my own will to live. And that had to be enough.

Then, a miracle.

A shift in the sky—a break in the clouds. Just enough moonlight to cast a faint glow over the water. And in that light, I saw them—they were coming back.

Summoning every ounce of strength, I waved my arms, kicking furiously against the waves. And this time, they saw me. The helicopter adjusted, dropping a rescue swimmer into the ocean. I felt the grip of strong hands, the harness being secured around me. As they hoisted me up, my body hurt, the adrenaline crashing. I had survived.

That night taught me something I have carried ever since. Leadership is not just about planning and precision. It's about resilience. It's about making decisions when everything goes wrong. It's about pushing past the limits you thought existed, about refusing to surrender, even when the odds are stacked against you.

Survival isn't just about strength—it's about mindset. It's about knowing that no matter how dark, how hopeless, how impossible the situation may seem, there is always a way forward. You just have to keep treading water long enough to find it.

THE POWER OF A LEADER'S VOICE

A leader's voice carries weight far beyond the words they speak. It has the ability to uplift, ignite passion, and create clarity in times of uncertainty. Leaders who communicate well don't just relay information; they inspire action. They understand that in order to scale successfully, they must win hearts and minds, not just execute a tactical plan.

Great leaders—whether in business, politics, or social movements—have always been great communicators. Think of Steve Jobs unveiling a new Apple product or Oprah Winfrey galvanizing millions with her message of empowerment. These individuals don't just inform their audiences—they ignite excitement and create an emotional connection that makes people want to be part of something greater than themselves.

WHY MOTIVATIONAL SPEAKING IS CRITICAL FOR SCALING

As organizations grow, complexity increases. Teams become more distributed, priorities shift, and maintaining alignment becomes more challenging. A leader who can effectively communicate their vision ensures that employees remain engaged and focused, even during rapid change. Without clear, inspiring communication, scaling efforts can feel disjointed, and employees can become disengaged, leading to inefficiencies and setbacks.

Leaders also need to motivate external stake-holders. Investors must be convinced that the company's growth trajectory is solid and worth backing. Customers need to feel a deep connection to the brand in order to remain loyal. Industry partners must believe in the organization's direction in order to collaborate effectively. In every aspect of business growth, the ability to articulate a vision with clarity and passion plays a crucial role in driving support and engagement.

THE ART OF STORYTELLING IN LEADERSHIP

Storytelling is one of the most powerful tools in a leader's communication arsenal. Facts and figures are important, but stories make those facts meaningful. Stories create emotional connections, help people retain information, and make abstract ideas tangible. Leaders who use storytelling effectively don't just present their ideas—they make them come alive.

A compelling story has three essential elements: a relatable protagonist, a challenge or conflict, and a resolution. In business, this could be the story of the company's founding, the hurdles overcome along the way, or a customer whose life was changed by the product or service. When leaders weave narratives into their speeches, they make their messages more memorable, engaging, and persuasive.

MASTERING PERSUASION AND INFLUENCE

Motivational speaking is not just about inspiring—it's about persuading. Effective leaders understand how to craft messages that influence decision-making, drive commitment, and encourage action.

One key principle of persuasion is knowing your audience. Employees, investors, and customers have different priorities, concerns, and aspirations. A strong leader tailors their messaging to resonate with each group. Employees may need reassurance and direction; investors need confidence and data-backed projections; customers seek authenticity and trust.

Another critical aspect of persuasion is confidence. People are more likely to believe in a leader who believes in themselves. Leaders who speak with conviction, passion, and authenticity build credibility and inspire loyalty. They also understand the importance of body language, tone, and pacing—elements that can make or break the impact of a message.

SPEAKING WITH CLARITY AND PURPOSE

Motivational speaking is ineffective if the message is convoluted or vague. Clarity is key. Leaders must distill complex ideas into simple, digestible messages that resonate. The best speeches are concise, direct, and free of unnecessary jargon. They focus on what matters most and leave audiences with a clear understanding of the leader's vision and next steps.

Purpose also plays a crucial role. Every speech or message should have a defined goal—whether it's to inspire action, drive alignment, or instill confidence. Leaders should ask themselves: *What do I want my audience to think, feel, and do after hearing this?* By starting with the end in mind, leaders can craft compelling and actionable messages.

MOTIVATING THROUGH CRISIS AND UNCERTAINTY

During times of crisis, a leader's words become even more critical. Employees look to leadership for reassurance, stability, and direction. A poorly delivered message can cause panic, while a well-crafted one can unite and strengthen teams.

In times of uncertainty, honesty is paramount. Leaders should acknowledge challenges rather than downplay them while also instilling confidence in the organization's ability to navigate difficulties. Transparency builds trust, and trust fosters resilience. The most inspiring leaders don't just motivate in good times—they provide a sense of purpose and resolve in the face of adversity.

BUILDING A SPEAKING PRESENCE

Becoming an effective motivational speaker isn't just about what is said—it's about how it's said. Leaders with a strong presence command attention, engage their audience and leave a lasting impact. Developing a compelling speaking presence involves:

- **Authenticity:** Speaking in a way that feels natural and genuine. Audiences can sense when a speaker is being insincere.

- **Energy:** Using voice modulation, gestures, and movement to create a dynamic and engaging delivery.

- **Connection:** Making eye contact, engaging with the audience, and reading the room to adjust tone and pacing.

- **Preparation:** Knowing the message inside and out makes delivery feel effortless and confident.

PRACTICAL WAYS TO IMPROVE MOTIVATIONAL SPEAKING

Great speakers aren't born; they are made. Leaders can develop and refine their speaking abilities through consistent practice and feedback. Some practical ways to improve include:

- **Rehearsing Regularly:** Practicing speeches out loud, recording them, and analyzing areas for improvement.

- **Studying Great Speakers:** Watching TED Talks, keynote speeches, and successful business leaders to learn techniques that make their delivery effective.

- **Engaging in Public Speaking Opportunities:** Volunteering for panels, presenting in meetings, or joining groups like Toastmasters to refine public speaking skills.

- **Seeking Constructive Feedback:** Ask mentors, colleagues, or communication coaches for honest critiques and actionable improvements.

THE LEADER'S ROLE AS CHIEF MOTIVATOR

A leader's ability to inspire through speech is critical to scaling successfully. Without strong communication, even the best strategies can fail due to a lack of engagement, alignment, or belief. Leaders who master the art of motivational speaking create organizations that are not only driven by vision but also by purpose and passion.

Whether rallying a team, securing investor confidence, or winning customer loyalty, communicating persuasively and authentically is a non-negotiable skill for leaders who want to scale smartly. The best leaders don't just give speeches—they move people to action.

13

LOOKING AHEAD

E ffective leadership is the driving force behind a business's ability to scale successfully. Scaling is not just about growth—it's about sustainable, strategic expansion that maintains the company's core values and vision. Without strong leadership at the helm, an organization can quickly lose focus, veering off course amid the complexities of rapid expansion. Leadership provides the clarity needed to set ambitious yet achievable goals, ensuring that every decision aligns with a long-term roadmap for success. Without this guidance, even the most promising businesses risk becoming overwhelmed by the chaos of unchecked growth.

One of the most critical responsibilities of a leader is shaping and preserving the organization's culture. Maintaining a cohesive and value-driven culture becomes increasingly difficult as a company scales, yet it is essential for long-term success. Leaders who actively reinforce core values ensure that employees remain aligned and motivated, even as teams grow and operational complexity increases. A strong culture provides consistency in decision-making, fosters accountability, and unites employees under a shared mission, allowing the business to expand without losing its identity.

Equally important is a leader's role in driving innovation and continuous improvement. Scaling is not a one-time event but an ongoing process that demands adaptability. Market conditions shift, customer expectations evolve, and new technologies emerge. Companies that fail to innovate during their scaling journey often stagnate or decline. Strong leaders create an environment where employees are encouraged to think creatively, challenge the status quo, and embrace calculated risks. This commitment to innovation ensures that the organization remains competitive and responsive in an ever-changing landscape.

However, leaders must also be wary of **creeping excellence**, the dangerous tendency to continuously raise the bar for selection and performance in a way that ultimately excludes strong talent. While setting high standards is important, organizations that continuously shift expectations without clear justification risk alienating potential contributors and stifling progress. Effective leaders recognize the balance between maintaining high performance and ensuring inclusivity, making it possible for top talent to grow alongside the company rather than being squeezed out by ever-increasing demands.

People are the most valuable resource in any scaling business, and strong leaders understand the importance of attracting, developing, and retaining top talent. Scaling brings increased complexity, requiring skilled individuals to manage growing responsibilities. Exceptional leaders invest in their teams by fostering a culture of learning, mentorship, and professional development. They ensure employees have the tools and support they need to succeed, creating an environment where talent flourishes rather than burns out under pressure. Leaders build organizations that can scale sustainably without losing momentum by prioritizing their people.

Resource management is another critical leadership responsibility during scaling. Growth requires careful allocation of financial resources, technology, and human capital. Mismanaged resources can lead to wasted expenditures, operational inefficiencies, and financial instability. Strong leaders take a strategic approach to investments, ensuring that every dollar spent aligns with the company's growth objectives. They also recognize when to scale operations, when to pivot, and when to pause to refine existing processes before taking the next step forward.

With growth comes risk, and effective leaders are skilled at identifying and mitigating challenges before they become major setbacks. Scaling introduces new vulnerabilities—financial, operational, and cultural. Strong leaders cultivate a **risk-aware culture**, encouraging teams to anticipate potential obstacles and develop contingency plans. By implementing robust risk management practices, they ensure the business remains stable and resilient, even during periods of rapid expansion. Leaders who proactively manage risk position their organizations to weather challenges without derailing long-term progress.

As organizations scale, communication and collaboration become increasingly complex. What worked in a small, close-knit team will not necessarily translate to a larger, more dispersed workforce. Leaders are crucial in ensuring communication remains clear, open, and transparent. They establish systems that allow information to flow smoothly across departments, preventing bottlenecks and misalignment. Additionally, they foster a culture of collaboration where teams work seamlessly toward shared goals rather than operating in silos. Effective communication enhances efficiency and strengthens trust across the organization, which is essential for sustaining momentum during growth.

Above all, scaling smart requires a relentless focus on the customer. Expansion should never come at the expense of customer satisfaction. Strong leaders emphasize a **customer-centric approach**, ensuring that the organization continues to provide value even as it grows. They instill in their teams the importance of listening to customer feedback, adapting products and services to evolving needs, and maintaining the personalized experience that made the company successful in the first place. Customer loyalty is one of the most powerful drivers of sustainable growth, and leaders who prioritize it set their organizations up for long-term success.

Ultimately, **leadership is the foundation upon which scaling smart is built**. It is what holds together the vision, the people, the strategy, and the execution. Scaling is a test of leadership, requiring vision, adaptability, strategic decision-making, and a commitment to continuous improvement. Leaders who understand this—who see growth not as a chaotic sprint but as a structured and deliberate process—are the ones who build businesses that don't just expand but endure.

9 781963 701463